let's have a banquet!

let's have a banquet!

JOYCE LANDORF

Illustrations by Nona Lamb

ZONDERVAN PUBLISHING HOUSE

GRAND RAPIDS, MICHIGAN

Grateful acknowledgment is made to

MOODY PRESS, Moody Bible Institute of Chicago, for permission to quote two poems by Martha Snell Nicholson from *Her Best for the Master*, copyright © 1964 by Martha Snell Nicholson.

ZONDERVAN PUBLISHING HOUSE for permission to quote from *The Amplified Bible*, copyright © 1965 by Zondervan Publishing House.

Dedicated to

Dick Landorf
My president, my chairman and
my husband

Preface

Oh Joy — it's May again! I say that with a mixture of acute pain and memorable pleasure. May brings flowers, showers (the bridal kind too), May Day and Mother's Day and I am told that florists all over the United States have their biggest month in May. And for five years now, something else happens in May and it happens to us. Talk about being where the action is, or taking part in a "happening," we get it in May and get it good — and no "happening" could ever be quite as exciting!

I've never kept actual count of all the singing and speaking engagements I do each year, but with the coming of May I do know that in a six-week period I sing and speak at some 25 mother and daughter banquets. With that many banquets in that short a time, we resort to planned neglect instead of housekeeping, we wear out one set of tires, and we do indeed, suffer from tired blood, body and bones.

You can imagine with my going to that many dinners, luncheons and teas, it gets pretty hard to have our family fun and talks around our dinner table. So we begin our yearly communicating in notes, letters and scribbles of all sizes. My husband's handwriting is so horrible that by the time I've figured out *what* he said to do, it's too late. Rick, our teenage son, switched to printing as soon as he (and I) discovered he had inherited his father's illegible hand, and his notes are usually brief but warm. Laurie, our twelve-year-old, loves any excuse for writing a note, and since she always gets an "A" in penmanship, her notes are pure joy. Then, there are a whole host of communiques from friends, neighbors, mailmen, delivery boys and one sweet note from the Salvation Army men. (They came twice to pick up some old clothing and missed me; but as they said, "No hard feelings.")

In front of me are two notes from Laurie. The first note was pinned to the front door so I would not miss it when I came home from a banquet, and it reads:

> Dear Mommy,
>
> Guess what, I had to go to bed at 8:30 (Daddy's orders) because of the field trip tomorrow! Lynn came over and said to wear pants tomorrow. Make me a good lunch! Not that you never do . . . but roast beef please!!!
>
> XXOO Laurie

I made her lunch, including a roast beef sandwich, late that night so I could sleep in the next morning. When I awoke I found this note taped to the coffee pot. (That girl uses more tape in May than all the rest of the year put together.)

> Dear Mommy,
>
> I wore my bell bottom outfit. I didn't want to wake you up. I really love you a lot. I can't write very good, the dog is biting on the pen . . .
>
> (unsigned. I guess the dog got to her.)

There are many other notes from her and the rest of the family like this one from my husband Dick, who affectionately calls me "Mrs. Dorf" and signs all his cards, letters, etc. "Mr. Dorf." This was scribbled on the edge of a letter from a program chairman:

Darling,

Now that they have changed dinner to dessert, what time will it begin?

Mr. Dorf

Another note said simply and directly (if not tersely), "Hon, you *must* go to the bank TODAY."

The notes from Rick are rather direct and to the point, but his signature always makes me glow. I found this note pinned to his pants in my sewing room:

Dear Mom,

Please fix these pants like you did the other ones.

XXXXOOOO

To all these notes we add *my* notes of instruction, menus, directions, threats and encouragements, all geared to keeping a family whole, well and happy during the merry month of May. Each night before I leave, the meal is hot and ready to go, the children have their various jobs, and when Daddy gets home, dinner is served. (I've based all this planning around the old tradition that if my husband does not have a clean white shirt, the children are not happy, and if the whole family does not have a hot meal each night, I'd better not go to a banquet and tell other mothers how to make it as a mother.)

Since I have very little sense of direction (would you believe none at all?) my notes to Dick are usually about "How do I get there from here, or can I?" One of my notes tells the story —

Darling,

Does this lady mean turn left when she says "south"? Also, speaking of south, why is it at the *top* of her map?

Mrs. Dorf

By now you're probably asking yourself why we go to all this trouble. Why not just take a small number of engagements (I *am* taking fewer next year) and, if I like my home and family so much, why not stay home completely? The answer is simple, but yet like all simple answers, it goes very deep. You see, we almost missed God's unbelievable, miraculous plan for our lives as a man and a woman and as a family. How God reached down and became our forgiving Saviour, and where we were when it happened, has introduced many hundreds of people to the Lord, and we have watched as He has bound together broken, despairing marriages like ours. So, we keep up this hectic pace for these six frantic weeks. It can all be summed up very well in a note from a friend of mine who was stopping by for her coat. I had to be gone, so I left this note for her:

> Dear Ruthie (and Eleanor),
> I meant to have you look the other day, but forgot — Go see my roses — isn't God smashing?!!!
>   XXOO Joyce

I have seventeen tiny rose bushes just outside my dining room glass doors, and the roses were in full, bursting pink bloom. Ruth's note back said:

> Dear Joyce,
> We did . . . and He is!

This note not only sums up God's greatness to us, but the whole wild month of May. Oh, all those wonderful banquets! I should share them with you! In fact, I shall!

On the following pages are some of the exciting, sometimes unbelievable experiences that have happened in this merry, merry month of May.

Now I couldn't have all these rich experiences if it were not for all the program chairmen I meet by the dozens. You see, in this one month alone, I finally come into personal contact with some 20 to 25 program chairmen, after months of writing, telephoning and switching dates. They are a most admirable group of ladies and I have learned a whole series of lessons from them; in fact, enough to fill a small book!

My thanks to a loving family,
praying friends, working secretaries
and fascinating chairmen

Contents

let's have a banquet!

I

The Chairman

or "Mrs. Smith, you have just volunteered!"

It doesn't always happen this way, but I think a good rule of thumb would be for you to remember this bit of advice: Never stay away from the meeting at church the night elections are being held! This is one excellent way of getting yourself voted in as chairman by some dear soul who explains the whole thing away by saying, "Let's elect Susie; she'll be glad to serve. Besides, she isn't here to object." Congratulations are in order then because you have just been "volunteered."

Program chairmen come in all sizes and shapes. I've known big creative ones, little zippy ones, middle-aged and young ones, cute ones, unattractive ones, elegant ones and homespun ones, but all of them are marvelous! Some are quiet yet efficient, others loud yet not demanding, some handle their job with an "iron-hand-in-velvet-glove" attitude, and some must have gotten their training for the job in the army. But all have one trait in common — it's usually portrayed differently by each gal, but it's always there: *nervousness.*

Nervousness

I've noticed that nervousness is no respecter of persons. It hits the gal who has planned and plotted out a banquet course for a year as well as the gal who stepped in at the last moment to replace someone, the one who has worked her fingers to the bone, and the one who planned the program the night before. So expect to be nervous, then make it work for you. I heard an Academy Award winner answer the question about jittery nerves. He said, "Anyone who says they are not nervous on stage is a liar. We are all nervous and when we are not, we are overconfident and that's when we really mess up."

Remember, all the cells are really going. Your heart starts pounding like a sledge hammer the moment before you stand and say, "Good evening, ladies." Your pulse shoots up and generally you are tired and tense. With this excessive burst of power running through your veins you are likely to forget your first name. (Write it down. You may want to use it.)

My friend Ruth was counseling a lady on this very subject. The lady said she had prayed for God to remove her fear and nervousness, yet each time she participated in a program, her stage fright remained and was overwhelming. Ruth reminded her of II Corinthians 4:7: "But we have this treasure in earthen vessels, that the excellency of the power may be of God, and not of us."

Perhaps the reason stage fright, fear and nervousness never completely leave is just one of the unique ways God has found to remind us we are earthen vessels and all power is God's — not ours!

Also, this about nervousness — don't mention it. Especially to the public. Anyone who has experienced public speaking knows all about those knocking knees, sweaty palms, dry throat and temporary memory losses you're experiencing. If they haven't done any public speaking, they probably won't notice you. That's kind of humiliating when you think about it, but people tend to take in the whole scope of the program rather than singling out one certain person. It will be a discredit to you if you rattle on about how late you are because the starter on your car broke, or how mad you are with the cook, or that just now you saw fifteen people arrive and they don't have reservations! You accepted the position of chairman, at least for this year or this program, so live up to it. No matter what happens, take it in stride. This is easier said than done, but if you have honestly done your homework, worked and prayed with your committee and then everything falls apart the last second, what can you do about it except use an alternative?

I have a friend who says there *are* no problems, only solutions. So when your first vice-president tells you she has just received a call from the caterer, their food truck has broken down and dinner will be an hour late, tell her, "No problems, only solutions." Then begin your first half of the program as if you planned it that way all along. As I think of it, having some of the program *before* dinner might just be a great idea and a welcome change.

Sense of Humor

We all know about the five senses: touch, taste, smell, hearing and sight. But as a chairman you are going to need three more — starting with a sense of humor!

Show me a chairman who takes herself and everything

that happens to her very, very seriously and I'll show you a gal without a sense of humor. She will be very difficult to work with and even more difficult to please. Her serious heart will be the exact opposite of the Scriptures' merry heart, and when they say, "A merry heart doeth good" (Proverbs 17:22), this gal's heart will work the opposite.

I remember a chairman with a great sense of humor even when I nearly ruined the ending to her marvelous program. She surprised me just after I had sung and spoken, by asking me to lead the audience in singing "Blest Be the Tie That Binds." I was a little numb due to my 45-minute-program fatigue, and for the life of me, I couldn't remember how the melody went! I stood there looking like some kind of an idiot. Quickly she came laughingly to my rescue and said, "Would you believe 'Doxology'?" Fortunately the words and melody to *that* one came and we have laughed over the incident several times since.

Somehow we keep forgetting that as Christian women we have the Holy Spirit's help and by His fruits we will be known. If the second fruit of the spirit is Joy, then we *must* let the Lord channel it through us. We stand yelling to the world, "Hey, look at me, I'm a Christian peach tree; I have love, joy, etc., etc." The world looks back at us (especially when we are crestfallen because our program did not go right) and says, "If you're such a great peach tree, how come you're only bearing lemons?" That is a point! The Scriptures remind us that we will be known for the fruits we bear.

When worst comes to worst, it is not the end of the world (even though you may wish it were), so put up both chins and smile.

22

Sense of Forgiveness

Women's organizations are notorious for not forgiving. Rather I should say they might forgive, but forget? *Never!* You find this in the P.T.A., the hospital auxiliary, the women's club and yes, even in the ladies' missionary society — shall we say, particularly in the ladies' missionary society? We seem to keep losing sight of the fact that the work of God will go on for His glory, with or without us. There is always the little feeling that we are quite indispensable to God's work. The second our feelings are hurt (sometimes we let the hurts pile up a little just to be justified), we let it be known, "I'm not going to give of myself and do such-and-such because so-and-so said that-and-that!" Usually our unforgiving attitude is pointed out by some kind soul (we don't like her either), and by then we really compound the fracture by *never* forgetting or letting it heal.

I wish the verse in Ephesians 4:32 (Amplified Version) was not quite so clear. We could get around it a little better. However, it doesn't say that we must merely forgive old so-in-so, it says clearly, we must "become useful *and* helpful *and* kind to one another, tenderhearted (compassionate, understanding, loving-hearted), forgiving one another [readily and freely], *as God in Christ forgave you.*" By the way, have you noticed I've used "we" on this subject of forgiveness? I'm speaking to myself as well as to you chairmen. The Lord has provided many opportunities to test my ability at forgiving (really forgiving) some strange, strange people. One such test came at a banquet last year.

I arranged, as usual, the entire dinner for my family, left all the right notes, showered and dressed and then set out one hour early for the 6:30 P.M. banquet over fifty miles away. I was soon tied up in the occupational hazard known to the freeway traveler as the "bumper-to-bumper routine" but I managed to survive both the freeway and the inadequate directions I had been given, and I arrived promptly at 6:30 P.M. As I whizzed into the parking lot I realized with some degree of horror that it was completely empty. *Oh boy*, I thought, *I've finally done it! I've come to the wrong church on the wrong night at the wrong time.* (I have nightmares in May about this sort of thing.)

Just to be sure though, I went into the church. It was empty, but tables were set up and I could smell food cooking. Then I saw a lady, and to my surprise, she was the chairman. When I introduced myself, she said she was pleased to meet me, and told me how much she was looking forward to hearing me.

I mumbled, "Tonight?"

"Oh, yes, tonight," she answered.

I was quite puzzled and managed to say, "No one is here and I wonder if I understood your letter correctly, you *did* say 6:30?"

You probably won't believe this, but as cool as a mountain stream she said, "Oh, yes, we told *you* 6:30 P.M. so *you* would be on time. Actually, we won't be ready to start until 7:00 or 7:30." (It was 7:42 P.M.) I guess she had had some trouble with speakers arriving late and was taking no chances with me!

Out of 25 banquets this year, only one started exactly on time. I arrived at each one at the specified time and have waited for ten to thirty minutes. I generally spend the time remembering all the things I forgot, or could have done at home.

24

The chairman who made me wait over an hour last year was quite an exception to all the gracious chairmen I have known, but I remember as I waited in a small chapel adjacent to the dining hall, I found myself explaining to the Lord that I would *never* forgive this lady for making me leave home so early, go through peak hours of freeway traffic and then sit and wait for an hour. It seemed easier to bear after I admitted I could never forgive her. I soon found myself asking the Lord to forgive her *through* me. I sat back, relaxed, and watched Him change *my* attitude. It was one of my better programs and best learned lessons of my life. Admit you can't forgive and then ask Him to do it through you.

If there is one person in your life — mother, husband, friend, daughter, mother-in-law, minister, doctor or teacher — that you cannot (or will not) forgive, you will never know God's full plan for your life. You limit God to a small portion of blessings by an unforgiving spirit, and it's very sad to see because He has *intended* showers of blessings and rivers of victory!

The other night my secretary said, "Forgiving someone who is truly sorry is fairly easy, but it's really hard to forgive one who is *not* sorry." This was just the case with the chairman who made me come early — she had done it on purpose, her plan had worked, and she wasn't one bit sorry! How clearly the Scripture welled up before me, "Create in me a clean heart, O God; and renew a right spirit *within me.*" Forgiveness starts with me, my attitude, my spirit — not with someone else! If I am unwilling to let God's forgiveness flow through me to the person toward whom I feel bitterness, then I shackle His boundaries to small areas and I'm forever lost to the bigness of God's plan and love.

Sense of Wonder

It's a joy, a privilege and a lovely delight to sit next to a chairman who has all her faculties for a sense of wonder! Nothing seems to escape her, every good deed and personal sacrifice of her committee is duly recorded by her and she is filled to capacity with gratefulness. I say to her, "The decorations are just beautiful!" She answers back, "Yes, aren't they lovely, Sally did them." Then after she points Sally out to me, she tells all about Sally's talents and she glows as she talks. Later I mention the dinner and she tells me about Mrs. Smith who cooked it, how she lost her husband a few years back and now does all the church cooking, and she ends with, "I don't know what we would do without her."

You see, this chairman has chosen her committee wisely, and as she has worked with them she has shown her sense of wonder at *their* talents, so she has inspired them to do above and beyond their abilities. A valuable lesson is observed here, and it can be applied to every aspect of life: inspiring your husband, your children, your friends, your Sunday school class, etc., to do above and beyond. What a labor of love! What a joy!

Henrietta Mears said she would try to instill divine discontent into the mind of everyone who could be doing more than they were doing, not by telling them the pettiness of their life, but by giving them a great vision of things that could be done enthusiastically, passionately. She also felt no leader could have the respect of others without "impartiality and a feeling for equality." And so it must be with the chairman and her responsibility to her workers. She must encourage their talents and then work as hard as she expects them to work.

When I think about the "perfect" chairman, I visualize several marvelous women; all different shapes and sizes, usually nervous, but all with a strong, dedicated sense of purpose. They have worked hard and long, but they have not worked alone. They have never been a single, loner type person, but a *team member* with their committees. Most important, they have let the Holy Spirit channel through them:

Joy	(when smiling over something that seemed incredible)
Forgiveness	(when the hurt and criticism were unjustified)
Wonder	(just about the time everything looked bad).

The thrilling part to me is that when the banquet is over, all their hard work, love and prayers are *not* over. On the contrary, they have just begun, and only eternity will reveal all the results.

2

The Planning Committee

or "Let's not knock ourselves out this year!"

No program, banquet or musical cantata is ever the work of just *one* person, but rather of a whole collection of people with various skills. Yes, it *does* take a great coordinator, but unless she has a great committee, she's dead before she starts.

Enthusiasm

My choir director is fond of saying, "Our choir is as good as its weakest member," and how true that is! It's the same way with chairmen and committee members. A chairman is as good as her most *un*-enthusiastic committee member. My husband told me the other day that his bank has a saying that goes like this: "Enthusiasm always filters down from the top; it never wells up from the bottom!" So, as enthusiastic as you are, madam chairman, so goes your committee. Enthusiasm is one of the most contagious things I know, but it's got to start with you. Your suggestions may be met with coolness or downright rejection, but ask for opinions and helps. Then once you have all settled on theme, date, food, etc., be prepared — for you will be the pepper-upper, the settler-downer and the smoother-overer for the whole group. Don't be weary in well doing, for it pays off handsomely — especially if you try to have fun while you're at it.

The best example of an enthusiastic chairman and committee I have ever found was at a little country church. Let me just tell you about dinner, although I could go on and on about the entire evening. The 6:30 banquet was delicious from the salad to the dessert, and I asked for every recipe used. Great meals like this just don't *happen*. They are very carefully planned, and this is how they did it. The chairman asked each of her five committee women what they would like to have served at the banquet. Then, each Wednesday for five weeks they met at each other's house for lunch. Each woman cooked what she thought would be best. Then after they had tasted all the food and considered all the ideas, they voted on the final selection. Aside from it being the most delicious meal I had that year, the committee had. a ball at the five Wednesday luncheons. One committee member did confide to me, "The only drawback was the ten pounds I gained while trying to find the menu for tonight!"

The enthusiasm of the chairman had infected the whole group and it permeated the air the whole evening. I can recall it vividly each time I use one of those recipes.

Speaking of food, you may have an excellent caterer available and this is always fun. At one catered dinner this year, we started with a good, but plain salad and then went into a delicious main course of chicken (boned breast rolled, then dipped into batter and fried), green beans (generously sprinkled with slivered almonds) and scrumptious potatoes au gratin. Serving very good food is important as so many mothers at mother and daughter banquets are experienced cooks, and if they had wanted lumpy potatoes or warm salad, they could have stayed at home. (I'm kidding, but you get the point.)

One chairman learned, after one disastrous banquet, that the two most important things about the food were to have it *hot* and *plenty of it*. Remember these two things as your committee talks food, menus and price.

Many churches are moving towards teas, brunches or salad luncheons rather than evening dinner banquets, and I'm pleased to see it happening as it is sometimes much more convenient (time-wise). Certainly it seems more feminine and very much in keeping with a happy spirit.

I can't recall all the wonderful menus I've been treated to, but here are a few:

Brunch   10:30 A.M. to noon

Large fruit salad

Hot rolls

Coffee, tea or punch

The fruit salad was served to everyone on a large nine-or ten-inch plate. A fluffy piece of lettuce served as a liner on the plate and was topped with all kinds of fruit; watermelon cubes, cantaloupe balls, two prunes, pineapple spears, fresh whole strawberries, apple slices, orange rings and crowning the salad was a colorful scoop of raspberry, orange, lime or lemon sherbet. The rolls and coffee were hot and plentiful. The tables were covered with bright yellow, pink, orange and green paper cloths, and with the various colored napkins at each place, it was a sea of color.

Luncheon   12:00 to 2:30 P.M.

Chicken (or tuna) salad scoop on lettuce
Potato salad
Fruit cup
Relishes
Hot buttered rolls
Cherry cobbler
Coffee, tea or lemonade

The beauty of this luncheon is in the making ahead of time since most of the dishes can be done the day before. In this case, five ladies made the main chicken salad and they made it together in the kitchen of the church. This is very important as it's easier to keep the menu consistent. Five other ladies made the potato salad, and another five the fruit cup and relishes. The fruit cup was tiny and was served on the plate in a little paper cup. It was part canned fruit cocktail, topped with fresh pineapple and whole strawberries. Five more ladies took care of the rolls, beverage and cobbler. In this way some 200 women were served and fifteen of their own women prepared the food — most of it on the day before.

Tea   2:00 to 4:00 P.M.

Tiny tarts
Mints
Nuts
Coffee, tea and punch (especially if it's a hot day)

According to my *Better Homes and Gardens Cook Book*, "Teas should be the ultimate in exquisite detail."

32   LET'S HAVE A BANQUET

I personally think a tea is just about perfect for a mother and daughter function, and when it is given in a large, lovely home, it is most beautiful. If your church (or pastor's wife) doesn't have a silver tea service, beg or borrow (try not to steal) a couple. Use all the silver accessories you can find; candelabras, dishes and trays, and set the mood for loveliness with fresh flowers. The floral centerpiece for the main tea table should be done by an expert florist or your most creative gal.

The most beautiful tea I have ever attended was given in a large home and only two colors were used as decorations; pale yellow and white. The simplicity and beauty were exquisite. All over the house were beautiful bouquets of yellow roses and white stock, as was the centerpiece on the table. The tablecloth was sparkling white, candles were yellow and white, and tea cakes were adorned with tiny yellow roses.

Tiny tarts are a favorite of mine and I have served them many times for shower-teas in my home. They are made simply by using a pastry mix, cutting out circles of dough with a cup or glass, and fitting each circle over inverted muffin tin cups. I use the minature muffin tins and bake 5 to 7 minutes in a hot oven, cool and freeze. On the day of the tea, the pastry cups are filled with a teaspoon of raspberry, strawberry or apricot preserves or instant lemon or chocolate pudding and topped with whipped cream or left plain.

One other word on teas: Keep the food "finger food" so that guests will not have to cope with utensils or a balancing act. Oh, yes, and should you not have a lovely home available and you have to use the church, find the most comfortable room (lounge or carpeted Sunday school room), and then make your table a beautiful focal point by using flowers, silver and perhaps a net, organdy or satin tablecloth. A magnificent silver brocade cloth was used at one tea because the chairman was clever enough to buy eight yards of 45-inch material at a fabric sale for $1.00 a yard. She cut the material in half and sewed the long selvage edges together so it covered the table and hung to the floor.

Dinner   6:30 to 9:30 P.M.
Tossed green salad
Ham and noodle casserole
Fresh cooked green beans
Jello salad
Rolls
Apple cobbler
Coffee, tea or milk

Price is a big factor in what you can serve in a large dinner, so generally that brings us to chicken or ham as the main meat. A word of caution: fried chicken is almost impossible to eat unless you can bathe afterwards.

The most outstanding menu cooked by the ladies in the church and not by outside caterers, was that one in the country I told you about (the five luncheons to decide on menus). They chose ham because of price and general taste. However, they did not serve it in thick hard slices, but cubed with noodles, and in a delicious cheese, onion and green pepper sauce. They served a green salad first, but with the main meal came a small fruit jello salad. The dessert was easy to fix, yet tasty and the extra touch was given by adding chopped walnuts and raisins to the apples.

For a really different kind of banquet, try having a

foreign type meal. A Chinese dinner, Mexican, Italian (there's more than spaghetti — like chicken cacciatora), Hawaiian or Polynesian or a real Swedish smorgasbord, all catered by a specialty restaurant (or by you if you know how). Remember to decorate with the colorings and accents familiar to the particular country. (Chinese food tastes extra special when surrounded with delicate cherry blossoms and tiny fans for favors.)

So much for food. Let's go back to your committee.

Personalities

Pick carefully your committee gals or you will waste a lot of precious time straightening out ideas and making peace between members. You will need all your energy for the task itself, and besides, remember that a peace-maker is seldom liked, so it will be a thankless job.

Just a thought on energy. All through my years of singing, I have observed singers, professionals and amateurs, who go through all kinds of unnecessary movements and motions as they sing. Even when they sing with a group or choir, they move their head, shoulders and upper torso. Each time I see this great amount of nervous energy being misdirected, I wonder how they would sound if they channeled all that movement into the diaphragm and vocal chords. It seems such a waste of precious energy.

I'm sure Satan will not stop you and your committee from doing a banquet, but rest assured, he will try to misdirect your energy. Straightening out argumentative members and peacemaking are misdirected energy-stealers and Satan knows well how to use them.

While I waited for one mother and daughter tea to

begin, I started looking at the faces of the women and girls. Everyone looked so dressed up and darling; everyone, that is, except two women on opposite sides of the room. Their faces stood out from the happy faces around them as if they had neon signs pointing to them. I could hardly take my eyes off them; both were sullen and scowling, both at odds with the whole world, and both *obviously* were as mad as wet hens! It was so depressing, I decided to turn my attention elsewhere.

And that's when I saw the table decorations! They were gorgeous! Each table had fresh, beautiful flowers simply laid down the center on beds of fern. I said to the chairman, "I've just noticed how beautiful everything looks and I'm overwhelmed by the various kinds of flowers!"

She turned a little pale and said in a hushed voice, "Oh, please don't say anything about the decorations when you speak today."

"Why?" I asked. "They are so lovely."

"Well," she explained, "See the woman over there and *that* one over there?" (Ah yes, my two wet hens!) "They were my decorating committee, and they fought so over what theme, what flowers and what decor, they never got together on *anything*. I spent so much time on the phone trying to get them together, but nothing worked. This morning I went to a friend's house, gathered all her flowers and did the best I could."

This chairman had really done her best at peacemaking, but the two women would not make up, so she used her only alternative. You may find yourself in just such a position. A verse in James (4:6, Amplified Version) reminds us that the Lord will give "more and more grace," by the power of the Holy Spirit. James goes on to tell us that the Lord gives grace to those who are "humble-minded [enough to receive it]." The graciousness of the chairman that day certainly reflected the loveliness of God's grace.

One other word on personalities. Try to remember all your committee's personalities (and yours) will be subjected to criticism. There is always someone who can find fault or reason to criticize. About the only people we don't criticize are the dead — so if you are alive, a committee member or the chairman, expect criticism. Then once more you will have the opportunity to see God's Holy Spirit give you grace and you will probably grow several inches taller because of the experience.

I remember a letter from a radio listener of mine. She was very critical of my diction — "Your diction, at best, is very poor" — and she based her profound knowledge of diction on one year of voice lessons. I was furious with her lengthy letter, especially the "I tell you this in Christian love" part, but I was even more infuriated at my husband, because after *he* read the letter, he broke up with hysterical fits of laughter! I didn't see it as *quite* that funny. However, he helped me to regain my sense of humor and balance about my radio ministry by pointing out that in nearly three years of daily broadcasting, I had received only three or four such letters. He reminded me of my eight or nine years of vocal studies and my honor awards in speech and drama.

Past president, Harry S. Truman, once said, "If you can't stand the heat — get out of the kitchen!" (Actually, he said it a little more colorfully, but I'm sure you get the message.) Anytime you set out to do a job, remember there will be criticism. Take heart from Moses who had an entire nation of critics at his elbow.

Attitudes

At least one member of most committees has the "Let's not knock ourselves out this year" attitude. If this member has to drop out of your planning committee, for any reason, *let her*. Many things can be done simply, economically and still come out very beautifully. But when this committee member says, "Let's not knock ourselves out this year," she *means*, "Let's throw some food together on the cheapest paper plates, forget fussing with decorations, and let Mrs. Jones read the devotional she gave last year." This kind of attitude produces the worst possible kind of a banquet, but even more horrible, this attitude generally influences chairmen and committee members for generations to come. Then, just you watch as an innocent new minister's wife tries to put chopped nuts on a rather plain dessert and this gal smirks, "What are you trying to do, go fancy on us?"

Each year I've asked chairmen what they thought was the most important qualification for a chairman. Always their answers begin with "attitude," and I see the results of "attitude" at each banquet. It pains me a little to know that out of the twenty-five banquets each year, only ten will really be great. Do you know what makes these ten stand out? Yes, that's right, the positive, "Let's go all out this year" attitude.

Where the women have pulled together, worked hard with singleness of purpose, realizing that this event, more than any other, will be attended by unchurched and unsaved women — the results are marvelous and miraculous. A dull church basement turns into a spring garden, complete with waterfall. A gymnasium is transformed as white paper doves are hung in pale blue bird cages from the ceiling. Or that extra touch is put into the meal by adding sliced water chestnuts to ordinary creamed chicken and the salad is a gourmet delight as the lettuce leaves have a delectable crown of sautéed bacon bits. The name tag each woman receives at the door is adorned by a tiny, handmade paper rose or delicate plastic daisy and the table favor she takes home has been lovingly fashioned by many hands.

Is all this work? You'd better believe it! But when it's done for His glory and His honor, you have had the joy of planting the first seeds of salvation. Someone else may water, but stick around, the harvest is not far off! When you and your committee have the burning desire to have *God's perfect will accomplished*, He has promised to give you the desires of your hearts (Psalm 37:4). So set your goals to His heights, and even though the problems seem overwhelming, you can and will climb and climb until these heights are reached!

3

The Theme

or "Do we have to do that again?"

The first scheduled committee meeting usually begins with the question, "Does anyone have any ideas for a theme this year?" The silence that follows is sort of alarming because it doesn't really mean that no one *has* a single idea, but rather, who will go first and share a thought, a gripe or a speaker suggestion. Ask any ten women if they have any ideas and you'll get ten different reactions. The very clever chairman who has a list of questions on a piece of paper for each person to answer is two steps ahead of the general confusion well known to the first meeting.

Here are some random questions you could put on paper for your committee:

1. Which banquet stands out in your mind as best?
2. What was different about it?
3. What food did they serve?
4. What made it special?
5. What did you like about our program last year?
6. What problems need correction?
7. Have you heard an exceptional speaker you would recommend?

8. Listed below are some ideas for a general theme. Please check the one you like the best. (You can't imagine how much time this question saves — but it does require a lot of thinking for the chairman.)
   If you have a suggestion for the theme, please add it to the list.

One really gifted chairman I know hands these questions to her committee a week *before* the first meeting. Oh, to be *that* organized! By the first meeting, most of the committee has some pretty well thought out ideas to present. It's no wonder the banquets in that church get better every year. Those sheets are passed on each year to each new chairman.

Whenever we talk about themes, we find there seems to be two schools of thought. Some want only sacred and inspirational themes, and others want only secular and fun themes.

I can remember a photograph taken of my mother when she was about 11 years old. She was balancing delicately on the top of a high picket fence. This is about where I stand on this question of themes; in the middle and on the fence, but the most important word here is balance. To keep a balance between sacred and secular seems to be the only realistic way of looking at it. For instance, an all-secular and light fun program in this day and age of heartaches and sorrow seems in very bad taste without God's message of hope. On the other hand, an all-serious and sacred program with no lightness or fun can put the audience on the defensive (especially non-Christians) or ill at ease. The whole world is desperately hoping it will find love and joy, at least in Christians, but when it does not see too much of it at a banquet in honor of mothers and daughters, they slip into the very familiar conversation about "those hypocritical Christians who never have any fun." This is *exactly* the time and place to show our unchurched, unsaved friends and loved ones our thoughtfulness and love, our sense of humor and our joy!

The Fun Themes

The fun part or light touch of any program can be in the actual name. Here are some examples:

1. *Mother Goose*

Nursery rhymes were used as decoration on wall boards all around the room. They had cut up the big nursery rhyme books and glued them up to tell the story. Each table had a centerpiece depicting a different rhyme. They had encouraged their ladies to come in costume and prizes were given for the most original, funniest and prettiest. As I recall, the grand prize went to a mother and her three daughters. They all wore dresses alike (made by the mother), but by their headgear, you could tell mother was the "bad wolf" and the girls were the "three little pigs." Children's records were played all during dinner.

You may want to use a circus or zoo theme along these same lines. One banquet using the circus idea used helium-filled balloons tied with long strings. They taped the string every 12 inches to the sides of the table. The colorful effect was breath-taking. By using so many balloons, each child had one to take home. The program was called "The Center Ring," with the mistress of ceremonies called "The Ringmistress."

2. Hat's Off to Mom!

This theme was used in several banquets I attended and in one, they used real ladies' hats as centerpieces on stands made of wire coat hangers. (Never underestimate the versatility of coat hangers.) Another group of talented ladies made little doll hats with feathers and sequins (all very fancy) then tied them to small white tree branches placed on each table.

The head table had place cards made from a six-inch round cardboard circle with a two-inch round piece of styrofoam in the center and covered with velvet or satin. A ribbon and a tiny flower made it look just like a picture hat. The name tag was tucked into the band.

3. A Taste of Color

The girls of Westmont College, Santa Barbara, California, chose this interesting title because they modeled clothes from a high-fashion store and picked only the brightest and gayest clothes. It was a real taste of color! This mother and daughter brunch was held in a very colorful restaurant, so little had to be done in the way of decorating.

4. Old-Fashioned Memories

This banquet was a delight because I happen to love antiques, and everywhere I looked that night were very old, lovely antiques! The centerpieces were some kind of an antique bowl, wash basin or pitcher, and on one table was just an assortment of small picture frames.

The highlight of the evening was a fashion show of bridal gowns dating from as far back as 1890 up to the present year. I asked where they found all the gowns and was told, "We started early."

5. Fashioned for Living

This was one banquet I did not attend, but I think it must have been a marvelous evening, so I'll share it with you. Of course, every woman seems vitally interested in fashions. If you think not, just listen to yourself talk the next time you see a darling little three-year-old all dressed up for church. You say, "Hello, honey. My, what a pretty dress!" Then we wonder why she grows up so clothes conscious. Anyway, fashions *do* interest us whether we admit it or not. This entire evening was built around fashions and the main part of the program was a fashion show featuring their own women dressed in the clothes they had made. Nothing new here, but the wonderful twist at the end was each model coming back and telling in a three- to five-minute package what Christ meant in her everyday life. The testimonies had been carefully

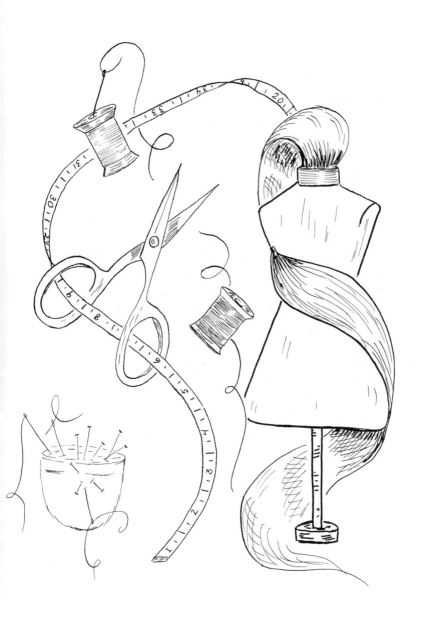

thought out, and no one ad-libbed away her allotted time. The effect of one mother sharing with another the adventure of being a Christian was most impressive and dramatic. This was all the early Christians had to say; "Look, this is what Christ has done for me." The women are still feeling the effect of those testimonies.

6. *Pattern for Living*

This theme has been used over and over again, and it is very good because of the balance between a light and spiritual touch. A small country church in Perris, California, used this theme one night, and the decor was outstanding. The dinner and program were held in a school auditorium that was lined with wall boards. These large boards had yards of fabric swirled and draped around huge paper scissors, pin cushions and other sewing aids. They had called a local Sears store and asked to borrow two life-size manikins, and to their delight, permission was granted — so, up by the piano stood two lovely well-dressed manikins primly posing the entire evening. A get-acquainted game played all during dinner was all about fabrics. The hostess of the table had a sheet with these darling questions:

Which Material Matches?

1. What is heard in a clock shop? (Ticking)
2. A prophet and one who falls for anything (Seersucker)
3. Good as cash (Checks)
4. How a chair should be used (Satin)
5. A picnic (Basket weave or outing)
6. What a fisherman uses (Net)
7. Fowls and me (Birdseye)
8. Two letters of the alphabet (Pique)

9. Kind of a worm (Silk)
10. A fraud and a donkey call (Chambray)

There were twenty-five all together and we had such fun talking and guessing. No one was a stranger by the end of dinner. Prizes were given to the table winning. Since there was a tie, they gave four more questions to settle the decision.

This same church the year before, used the following:

1. Ten points for each mother at your table and ten for each daughter she has with her. (Don't forget we are all daughters.)
2. Ten points for each grandmother.
3. Ten points for each daughter wearing patent leather shoes.
4. Ten points for each mother who had a baby during the last twelve months.
5. Ten points for each expectant mother at your table. (You may scoop the whole church and be the first to know.)
6. Ten points for each member who has had their tonsils removed and twenty points if it was this year.

The table decorations were very original and completely eye-catching. They took an old plastic detergent bottle, sprayed it gold, mounted it on a little dowel stick and wooden circle, and starting at the open top, draped it with a half yard of fabric, making it look for all the world like a miniature dress form.

Another chairman who used this theme found a sewing machine store manager who gave her several hundred little sewing kits. It was only a needle and pin set, but cleverly wrapped, and each lady had one to take home.

Incidentally, the fun touch at any banquet is getting to

take something home. During dinner at one church the chairman said, "There are some surprises for some of you if you find a red dot on your chair." It turned out every lady had a red dot, and between dinner and the program, they all went to a side door and received a little sample size perfume, lotion or some other beauty product. (A member of their congregation donated the samples.) The trip to the side door served as a welcome stand-up time for most of the ladies. These fun touches done *during* dinner really add the fun.

7. *Everything's Coming Up Roses*

This banquet was for 400 people, and much love, time and originality went into it The effect was breath-taking. When they wrote the theme title to me, I knew they would use roses and probably the handmade tissue paper kind, but I certainly was not prepared for some *6,000* of them. The long tables with white cloths had one double-decked topiary rose tree (almost 36 inches tall) and two single topiary rose trees (18 inches tall) on either side. One table used the deep blue and bright turquoise colors, another one the yellows and greens. Some trees were light lavender with deep purple, others were magenta red with pale pink, but each of the ten or twelve long tables had its own color scheme. Butterflies (made from matching tissue paper) stood on the tables around the trees.

The program (made of white parchment-like paper with an inset of matching construction paper) was adorned by a single tissue rose. The layout of the program was simple yet informative, and one of the best examples of good taste, so here it is, interspersed with my description of each item.

Waiters
Men's Brotherhood

When the dinner was ready, a secret signal was given to the waiters, and about 20 men marched up on the platform, towels over their arms, each carrying a paper platter. The piano gave them some good fast-walking music and when they all were on stage they launched into a rousing version of "Valdari, Valdara" with original words in the verse about the "roses they were privileged to serve." So that none of the men would miss any words, the lyrics were written on the paper platters.

PROGRAM

| Welcome | Kristy Denny |

The second all the waiters were back at their stations, an adorable three-year-old girl named Kristy, stepped to the mike and gave a quick poem (written for the evening) ending with the line, "Everything's coming up roses." The applause nearly took the building down, but when silence came, the blessing was beautifully given.

Blessing	Mrs. Bill Barber
Dinner	
Greeting	Mrs. Wilford Baker
The Rosebud Singers	

The Rosebud Singers turned out to be about 25 little three-year-old girls who carried nosegays of paper roses, sang two songs (including "A Rosebud, a Rosebud, Jesus Wants Me for a Rosebud") and ending with a verse about giving mother the nosegay — which they did.

LET'S HAVE A BANQUET

Mother-Daughter Look-Alike Fashion Show
Narrated by Mrs. Norm Rohrer

The fashion show was particularly lovely because (a) all the mothers and daughters were dressed alike and all the mothers had made the outfits. (b) They all came on stage, did a few turns and went off. They didn't try to go down crowded aisles. (c) It was 30 minutes long. Where you have a guest speaker and a fashion show, the show should not be more than thirty minutes. I sat through one banquet's 50-minute fashion parade and came quite close to simply standing and giving the benediction for my part.

Speaker and Vocalist	Mrs. Joyce Landorf
Pianist for Groups	Mrs. Bernard Travaille
Benediction	Mrs. Ronald Larson

This banquet stands out in my mind as one of the best I've ever attended, and a great amount of work, time and energy went into it. However, when a young teenager accepted Christ as I was speaking, nobody could have told her, her mother or her grandmother that "all that fuss was not worth it" — for it was!

I have given you only a few ideas and certainly you can enlarge on all I've said, but I hope this has given you a glimpse of the potential on banquet themes. In this particular age, women have all kinds of jobs, interests and hobbies that can give us a whole range of ideas in themes.

The light touch can be achieved not only by themes and decorations, but even in how the food is served. One church used all junior high, high school and college age men waiters, and it was hard to tell who was having the most fun the boys or their proud mothers! Another church used all the fathers. (Most churches find the men of the church very willing to repay the women for all the banquets they have served during the year.) They made quite a sight in dark pants, white shirts, red bow ties and vests made of red plaid oilcloth. The sides were stitched together, buttons were painted on with felt pens and the vests were closed by pins underneath. If you have a good leader, by all means have your men sing one number. Only one, because rehearsal time is short and it's better to have one good number than two poor ones.

The prize of all time, however, goes to the waiters of the First Baptist Church of Anaheim who waltzed in with 400 salads in their hands wearing the most darling pale blue ruffled pinafores you have ever seen. Some even wore wigs while others had a pony tail switch taped to their round bald heads. For all I know, they could have served salad for dessert, because I laughed the whole dinner time and still don't know what I ate!

Here's another happy, fun kind of idea involving all types of ladies. It's a fashion show (of a sort) and one church used only grandmothers for models. I've never seen such "hams." If they had any inhibitions, they were certainly well hidden, but perhaps that was due to the *type* of fashions presented. The narrator was very sedate and perfectly logical in her descriptions, but what appeared for viewing was another matter. Here are a few samples:

1. Plunging neckline dress — an ordinary house dress with a toilet plunger neatly tucked into the neck. A white toilet tissue hair bow completed the ensemble.

2. Combed cotton duster — a dress that looked like a dust rag with combs and cotton balls tied all over it. Skirt had a large whisk broom which the model used on her skirt and anyone else near.

3. Sack dress — a plain dress covered with large grocery sacks. Smaller bag was a darling hat.

4. Slip-over sweater — just that; a slip over a sweater.

5. Tea dress — plain dress with hundreds of tea bags hanging from it. The model carried a sign that read, "You're MY cup of tea."

6. A box suit highlighted by orange accessories — a large storage box with holes for arms and head. Real oranges were wedged in holes all over the front.

7. Simple little print dress — made entirely from newspapers.

These were all made by the ladies and made strictly for the fun of it all, and that's exactly what it gave . . . *much* fun for all.

Audience participation in some singing can be a delight, so be sure you have a peppy leader, be sure they stand while they sing, and don't let the singing go on too long. Included in the songs below is a fun song using knives and forks. Just remember to use it *before* the tables are cleared.

(Tune: "There Are Smiles")

Mothers sing

There are girls that make us happy,
There are girls that make us smile,
There are girls whose hands are always busy
And that makes the days seem more
    worthwhile;

There are girls that can make speeches
There are girls so capable and bright,
And these girls who fill our hearts
  with sunshine
Are the girls who are here tonight.

       Everyone (we are *all* daughters)
There are moms who make us happy,
There are moms who make us blue;
There are moms who are so very busy
Making "cash" for girls like me and you.
There are moms, and how we love them
  dearly,
Who have time for us both night and day,
And the mom I think is just a dandy,
Is the mom that God gave to me.

      (Tune: "You Are My Sunshine")

You are my daughter
  My lovely daughter
You are as pretty as you can be
  Your hair's so silky
Your skin's like velvet
  It is surprising just how
Much you look like me.

You are my mother
  My aging mother
You've been the best friend
  I ever had
You're cooking's the greatest
  Recipes the latest
You are the reason why
  I have this extra fat.

            — DALLEEN NEWMAN

FAITH OF OUR MOTHERS

Faith of our mothers, living still,
In cradle song and bed-time prayer;
In nursery lore and fireside love,
Thy presence still pervades the air:
Faith of our mothers, living faith,
We will be true to thee till death.

Faith of our mothers, loving faith,
For youthful longing, youthful doubt,
How blurred our vision, blind our way,
Thy providential care without;
Faith of our mothers, guiding faith,
We will be true to thee till death.

Faith of our mothers, Christian faith,
In truth beyond our stumbling creeds,
Still serve the home and save the Church
And breathe thy spirit thro' our deeds
Faith of our mothers, Christian faith,
We will be true to thee till death.

SILVERWARE SYMPHONY

(Tune: "Country Gardens")

You will need the following:

(1) *Knife in right hand*
(2) *Fork in left hand*
(3) *Two empty hands for clapping*
(4) *A glass in front of you*
(5) *A becoming whistle*

1. Knife on fork	8	counts
2. Knife on glass	8	counts
3. Knife on fork	8	counts
4. Whistle the tune	8	counts
5. Clap	8	counts
6. Knife on fork	8	counts

7.	Knife on glass	8 counts
8.	Whistle the tune	8 counts
9.	Knife on fork	8 counts
10.	Knife on glass	8 counts
11.	Knife on fork	8 counts
12.	Clap	8 counts
13.	Knife on fork	8 counts
14.	Knife on glass	8 counts
15.	Knife on fork	8 counts
16.	Whistle the tune	8 counts

(Tune: "Pack Up Your Troubles")

Stack up the dishes on the pantry shelf
And smile, girls, smile
While we were eating we enjoyed ourselves,
Smile, girls, that's the style.
What's the use of washing them?
It's hardly worth the while — so
Stack up the dishes on the pantry shelf,
And smile — smile — smile.

A SONG FOR LITTLE MOTHERS
(Tune: "My Bonnie")

My dolly lies still in her cradle,
I'm training her as I should;
My mother has told me about it
    And helps with her bringing up, too
Spinach — cereal
Will furnish her Vitamins B and C.
Food — sleep — fresh air
Will make her a big girl like me.

The Inspirational Themes

We need all the lightness and happiness we can get, as
stated on the previous pages, but if that is all we are

LET'S HAVE A BANQUET

going to offer then we may as well function simply as a social club. There is so much more involved. Through the years of May banquets I have watched God reach down, touch scores of women, and through that special touch, heal the brokenhearted, answer the questions of the bitter and meet the most burning needs of women today.

When I look at the May schedule and realize all the physical, mental and spiritual strain it will involve, my natural impulse is to shudder with exhaustion and cancel the whole business. But I can always remember the words of a friend of mine who speaks at many banquets when she said, "But the results, Joyce. How good God is!" To see so many trust Christ for the first time is the real importance here.

We must not be so wrapped up in our own world that we fail to see the need of a neighbor, friend or loved one. We must continually ask for God's wisdom and, having taken care of our own household, graciously present the good news of Christ.

Here are some serious or inspirational themes:

1. *In His Service*

One banquet last year used this theme, and to carry out the idea in the decorations, they had each table for ten decorated with either a lavender or a pink nylon net apron. The aprons, with their grosgrain ribbon ties, were tied to stands made of coat hangers. As far as you could see were these two beautiful colors of aprons. At the close of the banquet they were sold for 50¢ apiece, and while they were definitely serviceable, they retained a lovely femininity. Napkins on the white cloths were matched to the aprons on each table.

The short word of installation was based on God's word to Moses, "What is that in thy hand?" and we all came home feeling that even if it was only an apron in our hand, we would give it our absolute best.

One other banquet using this theme made their program menus on a small folded card covered with a piece

58

of material sewn on the top and a tiny ribbon as a band on a half-apron.

2. *Daisies Do Tell!*

So much can be done with daisies as they are easy to draw or paint. The spiritual application here of "Daisies Do Tell" is really contemporary, yet it fulfills the great commission given by our Lord so long ago.

Wicker baskets filled with real daisies were the centerpieces and everything was done in white, yellow and bright green. The programs and menus were large, white folders with daisies cut from yellow construction paper. The dark centers were black eighth notes, and green stems were drawn with felt pens.

One part of the program involved six women and a large (three feet in diameter) daisy. The center of the daisy said "Truth" then all six ladies took turns coming to the

daisy, picking off a petal and reading the appropriate scripture on the back. The petals were named; Love, Kindness, Humility, Honesty, Faithfulness and Patience. This would be a good chance to use some mothers who really deserve awards yet are never used or featured in public.

3. *Cameo of a Christian Mother*

I simply mention this one because of its potential. The banquet that used this theme made twelve-inch cameo faces out of resin and hung them in heart frames (made from coat hangers covered with lacy ribbon) on each table. The familiar Proverbs 31 was the Scripture base, but all through a program this theme could be used, particularly in the "Mother of the Year" presentation.

4. *Harmony With Christ*

Since this banquet used the talents of a real song writer, it really might have an edge on you, but some of the ideas used were very special.

The women had cut tree branches, sprayed them white and tied hundreds of little pink tissue paper rounds on them. When these tree branches were simply laid on the white table cloths it looked as if they had cut a hundred cherry trees down in full blossom. I thought I smelled them, they looked so real. (I think they *had* used a spray perfume.)

The "Prelude" on the program was a clever opening and welcoming speech using every play on musical words imaginable.

The "Sixteenth Notes" were two singing teenagers accompanied by two flute-playing teenagers. The sacred touch can be done so beautifully through music. It

could be a small choir of mothers or five little girls (ages five through seven) or even closing by all standing and singing "How Great Thou Art." Remember, too, that even the songs played on a record player during dinner can add that special touch.

"The "Offbeats" on this program were a mother and daughter tribute, but not in the usual way. The daughter, a gifted ventriloquist, gave her darling poem to Mother through the little dummy on her knee. Then her mother gave her tribute by singing a beautiful song called, "A Mother's Prayer" by Marjorie Chantrand. Talk about a balance in programing, this was it, for we laughed and giggled all through the daughter's darling poem and wept at the beauty of the mother's song.

Notice how the program was arranged.

5. *Precious Jewels*

I attended this banquet several years ago, before I ever thought of writing about banquets, so I'm sure I'll forget something vital, but it still stands out in my mind as one of the most creative. Certainly they used the Proverbs 31 chapter to its most imaginative capacity.

Every table for eight had a centerpiece made of someone's (real) jewelry chest, open and overflowing with all kinds of pearl strands, gold chains, earrings and pins — all set on a yard and a half of draped pink satin and flanked by a three-tiered candlelabra. Each table was a masterpiece of sparkle, satin and candlelight.

A word about candlelight: There is nothing prettier than eating by candlelight, but keep in mind that today our eyes are accustomed to high wattage light bulbs, and you may need more candle power to see sufficiently to dine. This banquet had used three candles at each grouping and since the tables were fairly small, it was very adequate. On the baby grand piano was a large old-fashioned trunk, open and spilling out jeweled treasures.

The programs were covered with sequins and scattered jewels (removed from a large assortment of old jewelry they collected for weeks) and printed on the cover were the words, "She is far more precious than jewels and her value is far above rubies or pearls" (Proverbs 31:10).[1]

I remember looking out over that audience of women and seeing their faces reflected in the candle glow. What sparkling women! They were truly more precious than any jewel!

[1]From *The Amplified Bible.*

6. *Love Letters*

This theme is perhaps the most original one in the group. The idea began in the heart of a creative gal, Edith Deverian, who attends Immanuel Baptist Church of Pasadena, California, and she simply took off on it. From tickets to the benediction, one was reminded of the Gospels and Paul's beautiful letters handed down for over 2000 years.

Brilliantly colored plumes used like giant quill pens were placed in resin bases and behind the speakers' table, a large wallboard had some wondrous words of Paul and some more quill pens. At each table place was a beautifully hand-scripted envelope. They had glued a used stamp in the corner and the letter was addressed to mother and daughter. Inside the envelope, instead of a regular printed program was this letter of love:

"THESE THINGS WRITE WE UNTO YOU THAT YOUR JOY MIGHT BE FULL" —I John 1:4

April 22, 1966

Dear Mothers and Daughters:

Welcome to our 1966 banquet, "Love Letters," which is given in your honor.

The Apostle Paul tells us, "Whether you eat or drink, do all to the glory of God." Tonight Frances Junker will ask the Lord to grace our table.

Please enjoy with us this evening's menu of mixed green salad, turkey breasts stuffed with dressing, glazed yams, broccoli, and cranberries; homemade bread and homemade apple pie. Coffee, tea, and milk, of course.

Since our children inspire us to express our love, tonight's fashion show will feature "A Mother's Labor of

Love." All the styles shown are home-sewn and the models are home-grown. Marjorie McBeth is our commentator.

At this point in our program we will have a little surprise.

Arlene Schoonhoven will introduce our guest speaker, Mrs. Joyce Landorf. "The Lord God has given me a tongue to know how to speak a timely word to the weary." (Isaiah 50:4)

To close our "Love Letter" we leave you with the words of John, "This fellowship of ours is with the Father and with His son, Jesus Christ." (I John 1:3)

In Christian love,
The Committee

On a separate card was this postscript:

P.S.

My own special thanks go to these gals for serving as a committee; Barb Witt, Carol Lagerstrom, Margaret Hamilton, and Marge McBeth. Many others helped out but naming everyone is impossible here.

The caterer was Linda's Swedish Inn and our genial waiters were volunteers from the Men's Fellowship.

Thanks also to Alexander Graham Bell for inventing the telephone. Without it, this affair would not take place until summer.

Edith Deverian

Even this fashion show had a spiritual touch as the minister's wife was the fashion narrator. She used the verse in Revelation in reference to "white raiment" and

Love Letters

Our Father's Garden

then told how she prayed for her children to be clothed in their hearts with the white raiment of salvation. It was a perfect introduction for a fashion show as it put the right emphasis on the right part; the heart first, the outside later.

I left this banquet full of the wonder of Paul's "love letters" to me and God's greatness!

7. Our Father's Garden

When you decide to have a program at your banquet without a guest speaker, you've hit on an original idea. You can use as many "flower faces" as you have little girls. I think this idea appeals to me because of its definite femininity. Nothing is lovelier than flowers, and a mother-daughter event seems to be just the right time to use them. Here is the program presented by Joyce Curry for Lincoln Avenue Reformed Church in Pomona, California.

OUR FATHER'S GARDEN

Decorations: A picket fence forming a garden is decorated with artificial flowers. Large tissue paper flowers are formed around a styrofoam ring, 12 inches in diameter. These fit around the face of each child (ranging in height). Each flower is described under the spotlight, then takes her place in the garden setting.

Spotlight on garden setting.

"The flowers appear on the earth; the time of the singing of birds is come . . ." — Song of Solomon 2:12.

> The gardens bring a greeting
> As flowers nod and sway;
> The birds sing happy anthems
> In a springtime roundelay!

The heavens are proclaiming
The wondrous power and might
Of Him who gives all blessings —
The Lord of love and light.
Our voices join the anthem
Creation sings today:
Praise the Lord, Oh praise the Lord!
For His blessings on our way.

— M. N. F.

Florists have a slogan, "Say it with flowers!" Everyone seems to like flowers, but they delight women especially.

Since we are now in the beauty of springtime, we will consider garden flowers as our theme this evening. Have you ever thought of comparing flower characteristics with human ones?

Flowers, like people, come in varied shapes, sizes, and colors. Also, like the human family, some flowers are hardy; some are fragile and delicate; some bruise easily; others flourish staunchly anywhere and are not readily discouraged. Even as the many nationalities which live in America have caused America to be called the melting pot of the world, flower gardens are a melting pot of color and variety.

Solo: First two verses of "How Great Thou Art."

What can we learn from flowers?

Spotlight on individual flowers away from garden.

The ROSE in its queenly beauty seems drawn from above, it is so fair. Yet we know a seed has died before there was growth, budding, and flowering. "Cut the blooms and enjoy them — they'll bloom all the more," a gardener spoke enthusiastically from his rose bed. Sometimes the Master Gardener prunes His human roses with disappointments, sorrows, and setbacks in order that they will turn to Him for strength to bloom more abundantly in life's garden. Roses, it is said, stand for love. "This is my commandment," said Jesus, "That ye love one another, as I have loved you."[2] True beauty radiates from within. Let us emulate the queenly beauty of the rose. "Let the beauty of the Lord our God be upon us."[3] We can be queens, not for a day, but *every* day as we tend and nourish life's choicest blossoms — the blossoms of love — in our own little corner of God's great garden.

Rose takes her place in garden setting.

"Consider the LILIES of the field, how they grow," said Jesus in one of His superb illustrations. "They toil not, neither do they spin: And yet I say unto you, That even Solomon in all his glory was not arrayed like one of these."[4] The lily is mentioned in the Bible as a type of a life of beautiful deeds and trust. Jesus bade us learn from the flowers God's loving care. Our Easter lilies blooming in the summer garden give us a lesson of purity. "Blessed are the pure in heart," said Jesus, "for they shall see God."[5] Only Christ can cleanse the heart of sin and make it pure and white and fair. Clothed in the dress of purity, lives become channels of blessing in the service of the Master.

Lily takes her place in the garden.

Duet: by the rose and the lily — "The Father's Care."

CARNATIONS! From early days of summer until fall, they splash their color in flower borders with a continuous outgiving of bloom. They are there ready to be cut to bring a riot of cheer into a sick room or grace a bowl for a festive touch to a pleasant dinner table. Little hands may pick a bouquet for Mommy or Grandma. Carnations give and give and give, their petals like grateful people giving thanks,

---

[2]John 15:12. [3]Psalm 90:17. [4]Matthew 6:28, 29. [5]Matthew 5:8.

but unless they are cut, they cease blooming. "Freely ye have received, freely give,"[6] says God's Word. May we be ready to give graciously of our time and talents that our lives may bloom out for Him in graciousness and constancy.

Carnation takes her place in the garden setting.

The appealing little PANSY with its velvety face is another lovely flower. "Pansies are for thoughts," and the pansy reminds us of those who have an abundance of inner richness because they have sown only seeds of goodness, kindness, and truth in the heart's garden. Daily they pray for cleansing of secret faults and yield themselves in obedient consecration to Him who is able to perfect them. "As he thinketh in his heart, so is he," and, "of the abundance of the heart his mouth speaketh."[7] Pansy-people have hearts washed clean. They have no room in their walk or in their talk for gossip or malice, but are ever kind and forbearing. Their lives reflect the sweetness of their souls.

Pansy takes her place in the garden setting.

A small brown bulb, drab, dry, without promise of beauty, is left to the elements — the wind, the sun and the rain, and God brings yellow sunshine to bloom in early springtime. The DAFFODIL radiates cheer. Can I, too, when there seems no apparent reason to believe cheer can come from situations, blossom forth as a light in a dark place? The gay daffodil has a mighty lesson to teach! "Be of good cheer," Jesus often encouraged. Trusting Him, we will be cheered in any situation.

Daffodil takes her place in the garden setting.

The DAISY in its white dress, with heart of gold, is the

---

[6]Matthew 10:8. [7]Proverbs 23:7; Luke 6:45.

simple flower of the countryside, giving of itself in friendly fashion without guile, or pretense. The daisy reminds us of the heart-of-gold folks who in simple, honest, dependable ways labor for Christ without thought of reward. Like the daisy, they share themselves freely in glad service and honest toil and prove "he that doeth truth cometh to the light, that his deeds may be made manifest, that they are wrought in God,"[8] as the Bible tells us. We need many daisies in life's garden plot.

Daisy takes her place in the garden setting.

"Plant these for color through heat and drought," urge the nurseries. "A small packet of seed produces a blaze of color." Our late summer gardens are "saved" by the ZINNIA. Don't you admire Zinnia-people? They are unruffled by heated, hasty pettiness. They are real flowers of brightness and sturdy faith amid the problems of the world of self-centered and unhelpful people. Zinnia-people labor, pray and worship, and their lives are a testimony of praise and strength along life's difficult pathway. "Endure hardness as a good soldier of Jesus Christ,"[9] says the Bible. Have we learned the lesson of the Zinnia?

Zinnia takes her place in the garden setting.

Beauty, purity, cheer, modesty, fragrance, hope, honesty, cleanliness, endurance, remembrance, constancy, seasoning — yes, the message of the flowers can grace our daily lives. The gardens praise their Maker. May our daily conduct be a tribute to grace our Father's garden plot as we bloom in His great garden of life! It takes many flowers to fill God's garden. Much care and work is needed to keep out weeds, pests and blight. Our lives, too, must constantly guard against

---

[8]John 3:21. [9]II Timothy 2:8.

evil, carelessness, indifference, and coldness. Every flower must be a bud before it bursts into bloom.

None of us would ever think of locking up our gardens so they could never be seen or enjoyed. And yet — without thinking — that is exactly what many of us do! I'm not talking now about the flower gardens that are so lovely at home. I'm talking about a very special kind of garden — the garden of prayer.

"After this manner," Jesus said, "pray ye"[10] — not merely in these exact words, but in this attitude of adoration, praise, dependence, submission, complete trust and faith. This is how we should enter our garden of prayer. Keep the gate open to your garden of prayer and let the fragrance of its beauty fill your life and the lives of those around you.

The Flower Garden sings "The Beautiful Garden of Prayer."

Spotlight remains on garden until program is finished.

Let us care most earnestly and prayerfully for the precious buds in life's garden — our own children — and nurture them until their lives gradually unfold into beautiful full-blown flowering.

Flowers lend brightness in sun or shower. Flowers turn for the sun's caress and warmth. We, too, receive heaven's graces when we turn toward the Light — Jesus, the Light of the world. One day, Tennyson, the well-known writer, walked in a garden among the blooms of many beautiful flowers, and a friend said to him, "Mr. Tennyson, you speak so often of Jesus. Will you tell me what Christ really means to your life?" Tennyson pointed to a bright yellow flower and said, "What the sun is to the flower, Jesus Christ is to my soul."

Flowers create harmony and beauty. They add a gracious

---

[10]Matthew 6:9-13.

touch of loveliness all their own. Each variety blooms happily according to its own nature.

So may we!

Solo: *Last two verses of "How Great Thou Art."*

8. *Transformed*

My letters from the chairman of this banquet said the theme would be "Transformed" but nothing prepared me for the fantastic evening that was in store for me. I was overwhelmed by (1) the decorations, (2) the installation of officers and (3) the tribute to mothers.

The decorations combined green caterpillars, beautiful butterflies and wicker baskets of paper roses. The fascinating caterpillars were made from one side of an egg carton

LET'S HAVE A BANQUET

turned upside down and sprayed a vivid kelly green, sequins glued on here and there and two black pipe-cleaner feelers. The pink and lavender butterflies, our programs for the evening, stood nine inches tall at each place. Inside were the several sheets of program. It was held together by the "body," "feelers" and "feet" of black fuzzy pipe cleaner. Every four or five feet on the tables were all kinds of wicker baskets filled with masses of paper roses of all different colors. Coming straight out of the top of each bouquet was a felt, sequined butterfly on a dowel stick. These butterflies seemed to hover over the tables. Place cards had tiny felt, sequined butterflies beside each name.

At the ticket desk each lady was given a paper rose corsage. The festive air created by the decor was just the beginning. In no other banquet have I seen the theme so beautifully used.

The first sheet in the program said: ". . . And be not conformed to this world: but be ye transformed by the renewing of your mind, that ye may prove what is that good, and acceptable, and perfect, will of God" (Romans 12:2).

Then at the bottom of that first sheet were the words to Audrey Mieir's lovely song "To Be Used of God," which was sung at the opening and closing. The actual program follows.

Dinner — (delicious) starting with fruit-filled orange halves made like little baskets with pipe cleaner handles and bow, followed by baked half capon. This was a little messy to eat with fingers, but the extra touch was given — each person had a "wet napkin" in foil for her convenience. Chocolate eclairs were the final delicacy. Immediately following dinner, before the program began, the chairman said, "Let's all stretch and look at the caterpillars and the butterflies." How important this is — to break up the sitting time.

Installation of New Officers — this is usually the place on the program we wish would be over quickly. Very often much time is wasted and there is an overall groan from the audience. The biggest mistake made is in asking a person to handle this part who has never done anything like it before. Way back in her memory she can conjure up a vision of the ladies coming forth one by one to light their candle from the big one, and so goes her installation (not very original, but very lengthy).

As soon as this part was reached on the program the pastor's wife asked the officers to line up quickly on the platform. (They did.) Then she gave the greatest installation sermon I've ever heard and she did it in less than four minutes. It went something like this:

"I looked up the word 'butterfly' in my dictionary and here is what I found. First, the butterfly has six legs. I thought then how we all need each other in the various tasks and how we all are needful of Christ. (She gave one appropriate Scripture verse.) But as I read on in the dictionary, I found that the legs are very inadequate, and I thought that even if we have each other, we need a greater help — our Lord. (Another verse.) Then also I found that as a butterfly flies he folds his first two legs. So it must be with all of you; before you fly, you must fold your hands in prayer or you will never get off the ground. Let us pray now in a moment of dedication."

It was so moving and true that I doubt I shall ever forget it. It was simple, to the point and quick.

Perhaps here is where I should say a word about "over-programing." Nothing kills the spirit of a good evening better than too much program. When we are in the planning stage it is easy to think, "Oh, my, what will we *do* for the whole evening?" Try to remember in those faraway planning months, that the evening will be a gathering for friends, family and guests — so right there is *half* the evening. Give them a chance to talk and greet friends during dinner. Most women I know are too busy raising families to spend much time socializing, so they look forward to a banquet and catching up on who has a new baby and where somebody has found a sale. (I learn about everything from who went to school to how to put in a new-type zipper.)

One or two banquets I have attended have had a special feature introduced during dinner. This works very well in Christian Business Women's Clubs because of the time factor involved, but at a main church banquet it can be disastrous. At one function they had a speaker who spoke for twenty minutes and then narrated a long fashion show all *during* dinner. The sound of her voice over the public address system, the clanging of the waiters' trays, and the unbelievable din of 300 people eating made one slightly hysterical. It was one of those rare occasions when, before I could speak or sing, I had to ask the audience for their attention. Actually, for what we had been through noise-wise, it was not surprising that it took some time to calm them down.

Back to the "Transformed" banquet. Next on their program was a short skit in two parts. It was called "To Be Used of God" and it featured a mother and her morning in a "before Christ" and "after Christ" transformation. It was built on the before and after life of one of their members and was simply a mother on the phone in the morning. The hectic, frantic pace of the "before" to the busy, yet ordered pace of the "after" was delightful. The best idea used in this skit was the pre-taping of the mother's words, all done ahead of time so she simply "mouthed" the lines. She did not have to memorize it, and because the tape was played over the public address system, we had no trouble hearing her. You could develop your own "before" and "after" script but again, keep it ten minutes or less.

Next came a very different fashion show; it was called, "Parade of Hobbies." It used only ten creative women in the church and very little time, but it was the real hit of the evening. The narrator began the parade by telling us that these were all things "transformed" by the creative ladies showing them.

1. A bag of scrap material became a quilt.

2. A plain pillow became a jewel of brilliance because of crewel work.

3. Plain plastic flowers were dipped and processed into a fragile "porcelain-like" arrangement.

4. An ordinary bowl became a vessel for a glamorous feather flower arrangement.

5. An artificial pineapple adorned with straw daisies became a darling conversation piece for the coffee table.

6. Plain gift boxes turned into glittering, velvet-covered and sequined-bowed packages.

7. A plain cake was turned into a basket of frosting and delicious tasting roses.

8. A white china plate was a work of art with its colorful hand-painted flowers.

9. A piece of plywood and a yard of burlap became a three-dimensional picture (a basket and plastic fruit almost real enough to eat).

10. A plain candle turned into a masterpiece by a handmade pink wax rose at its base.

After the women had presented their special hobbies for the parade, they displayed them out in the lobby and after the banquet answered questions.

A tribute to the oldest and youngest mother is always nice, but again, it is a time trap if it is not handled correctly. It comsumes so much time because most of us reveal our age *very slowly*. So, a good chairman has to have the right words or clever categories at hand. Sometimes it is good to find the oldest and youngest during dinner, for it avoids those long, long pauses between "Now let's see, who is over 68?" and "Well, find out if she's 84 or 85." By the time Mrs. Smith admits she's 85, had her daughter tell her what's happening (she's deaf), and has made her long trip forward to get the corsage, we are all worn out — and it's taken exactly 24 minutes. Be sure to have some darling young thing *take* the gift or corsage to the lady. At the "Transformed" banquet, the chairman simply asked who had a bee on their rose. (Remember the one we all got at the door?) Three ladies did and they were asked to come forward. One mother was the oldest (they had figured it all out ahead of time), one the youngest and one was a special honor of motherhood. They were given lovely gifts.

Another banquet chairman asked these unique questions and gave corsages to each winner:

1. Oldest mother who is wearing something she has made. (She turned out to be 74 and not only made

her dress but wove the fabric for her coat while dem-
onstrating an old spinning loom at Knotts Berry Farm.
How about that!)

2. Mother with the newest baby. (Two-month-old
daughter.)

3. Mother who has had the most children. (Once it
was eleven.)

4. Mother or daughter who has come the farthest.
(That's usually me, but I don't count.)

5. Daughter whose mother finished her dress closest to
the banquet time. (One hour before.)

6. How many family generations are here and wearing
something they made? (It turned out to be a darling
three-generation group.)

The traditional tribute to mothers and daughters is
usually a poem or speech by the daughter about the
mother and then *vice versa*. At the "Harmony With
Christ" banquet, the little girl ventriloquist gave the tribute, and at the "Transformed" banquet the minister's
daughter was another gifted ventriloquist. The delightful tribute below is the most creative idea that I have
heard. It was dreamed up by Joyce Curry of Lincoln
Avenue Reformed Church, Pomona, California.

*A mother and daughter are seen on the stage in the attitude
of prayer. The spotlight stays on them as they remain mo-
tionless throughout the narrator's comments. (You could
pre-tape this or simply have an off stage microphone, but
remember to have your narrator unseen.)*
Narrator: A Mother Talks With God

Dearest Lord, I wonder if all mothers feel the way I do
today. Tomorrow, a part of my life is going to end; my baby
is all grown up. I do hope she looks nice in her graduation
dress. Maybe the blue one would have been better. Now

isn't that silly of me, worrying over a dress, when I should be worrying about what's going to happen to her from now on. O God, I certainly hope I've done right! — that I've given something to my daughter to help her through the rest of her life. A little late now to worry about it, isn't it? But somehow I have the feeling that things will work out for the best. I guess that's the way I should feel if You are in my thoughts.

Dear me, but it seems like such a short time ago when Helen Rogers from the Guild peeped around the hospital and said, "My, that's a lovely little girl you have." Then she invited me to place Diane's name on the church baby roll. I had such a hard time keeping back the tears as we stood in the front of the sanctuary that day Diane was baptized — I always get so emotional over things. You know, it was almost a Sunday like this, with the sun making everything shine. Yesterday, when Diane was cleaning her room, I saw an old picture — of her first Sunday school class. I'll see many of them in choir today. It doesn't take long for those little ones of yesterday to grow into the young people of today. It's so nice that they had the chance to grow up together. You know, God, I am so glad that I chose You and the church to help me raise my child. If ever I felt myself narrow, selfish or lacking in understanding, somehow You were there to keep the light shining.

A Daughter Talks to God

(*Very reflectively*) It's a funny thing, but everybody on this baccalaureate Sunday is more concerned about my future than I am. "Diane," they all say, "we wish you the best of luck in the future." And "Oh, dear, she seems so young to be going off to school — hope she can take care of herself." Sometimes I feel older and more mature than they. Today I feel like singing hymns from the top of a hill — Just like saying, "Look out, world, here I come." Somehow, deep down inside — whatever the future holds, I know that You will always be with me. Today, in church, when everyone is praying for us, I think we should be praying for all of them, sort of thanking our families and the church for the faith they have given us through their witness. Yesterday when I went through all of those old pictures of me in the Baby Roll scrapbook, or me with all my front teeth out, singing in the choir; all of those snapshots from Sunday school picnics; the parties and plays of Youth Fellowship, and all of the other wonderful times we had. I remember those summers at church camp — prayer under the sky — and last summer at the work camp on the Indian reservation. Those are the pictures I like best. Guess it was about then that something happened inside and I finally accepted Christ as my personal Savior. All of the things that the church has given me, I want to share with others.

Thank You God for the senior retreats. It was there that we found ourselves truly sharing, helping, thinking, and loving, and most of all we found a greater understanding of You, God.

You know what, God, if I ever have children I hope I can do for them what my mother did for me in pointing the way to know You and Your only Son, our Saviour.

Whatever theme or tribute you decide to use, keep remembering that the work and trouble, time and money are well worth it! My mail continues to show that the Holy Spirit is still working and doing miraculous things even though weeks have passed since the actual banquet.

So, *go all out!*

4

The Speaker

or "A funny thing happened to me on the way to the banquet"

A question that still startles me even though I have heard it many times is, "How did you get started as a speaker?" and I never seem to answer it sensibly. The same thing happens when I'm asked, "How did you get started as a singer?" How does anyone get started in anything except to start? I have always been singing (at least I don't remember when I didn't sing), and even longer than that I've been speaking (so Mother said).

The day the first letter came from Zondervan Publishing House asking me to write, I said to my mother rather kiddingly, "Did you ever think your daughter would write books?" She smiled but gave a serious answer, "Oh, yes, I *always knew* you would write books." She then reminded me of a poem about Jack Frost. I had composed it when I was at the tender age of seven and very much in love with Michigan's winter season. Yes, I have always written. However there isn't a publishing house in the world that would have published my poem, but it was the beginning — the start.

This is precisely where speakers begin — way back — at first for just family, then friends, then small groups, and finally, with much experience, to many people and many groups. This is exactly why there are many speakers who are good, a few who are mediocre and a few who are excellent. It depends on their speaking experience, and largely on *what* they have to tell. (My heart has been so touched of God as I have listened to someone tell how they met Christ even though their grammar and speaking ability were almost nil. On the opposite side of the coin is the polished speaker who says everything just right, but has nothing to say.)

In the last five very active years of concert singing, public speaking, and daily broadcasting, I am still learning what it takes to be a speaker. I hope it never stops being a learning experience. It is an awesome responsibility and "To whom much is given, much is required." Let's look at some of the considerations in finding a speaker for your particular program and then the care and feeding of said subject.

Who?

Phil Kerr, although he knew almost every Christian musician in the world, rarely recommended any of them even though he was always besieged with requests for musicians. Once when I asked him about it he simply said that all too often the talent that would be excellent in one church would be terrible in another church. A trio would be received very well here, but at another church in the same city they would be seriously criticized. So he made it a policy not to suggest anyone. What he was saying was that not all musicians are versatile enough to size up an audience and fit into any irregularity that might develop.

Once, when Phil was taking me to a small church for a musical concert, he phoned me to say that he had just received a call from the pastor of the church. The pastor explained that his people really had a serious objection to anyone wearing lipstick and that if the singer was a lady, would she please not wear any. Phil called me then to ask if I would mind taking off all lipstick. (I never did wear too much, but I found people stopped asking me if I was ill if I wore just a little.) I felt that if it was this important to the pastor and his church, I could (and would) graciously take it off. I did, and the first thing Phil said to me when I got into the car was, "I think you look too sick to sing tonight."

On the way to the church he told me that I was about the only musician who would take the lipstick completely off for the sake of the congregation. Now, there are some who would argue that to take it off was hypocritical, but I've never forgotten the incident for it has served as a guideline for these past years of speaking. There are some issues that I cannot be moved on, but on some small things, as a singer and a speaker who wants God's will and direction in her witness, I want to the best of my ability, to be versatile and in good taste.

I have told you this little story about Phil Kerr to help you in your selection of a speaker. I could tell you "who" I think is a great speaker (we have some great ones on the West Coast), but in the last analysis, you will know your people, your church and your city best and you will probably be the best to decide on just the right one.

In your area there are several sources available to you to help you find a speaker. Probably the best source would be your pastor or his wife. They are constantly talking with other people and hearing various speakers, so they have more exposure to good speakers. Check first with the pastor.

Even if he doesn't recommend someone — still check with him. One very terrible experience I encountered was precisely on this point. The committee members *knew* their pastor would object to me (he did not believe in a personal God or that man is sinful) but they asked me to come in spite of him and give my personal testimony as so many of their women were in desperate need of Christ. As I began to speak (it was a mother and daughter banquet), I shall never forget the pastor's wife who was sitting just in front of me. Out of her large purse she proceeded to take several sheets of stationery, envelopes and stamps. Then, after she finally found her pen, she wrote a number of letters and completely caught up on her correspondence. (She didn't believe in sin either.)

Weeks later I was told that the pastor read a lengthy statement on the following Sunday to his congregation denouncing the speaker of the mother and daughter banquet and her theological views. The only consolation from that entire evening was that in the months to follow, many precious women who had been present that night were led to Christ later by a Christ-centered Bible class held in one of the homes. The seed had been planted during the banquet. The harvest was not far off. But the best policy is to check with your pastor.

Another excellent source of speakers is found in your Christian Business and Professional Women's Clubs of America. I'm not sure how they manage it, but they continually present excellent speakers and always seem to have a reservoir of the names of talented ladies in their files. I'm sure they will give you several leads.

Living on the West Coast and being a board member of Campus Crusade for Christ, I am very aware of the talented speakers in this organization. Contact your local Campus Crusade representative and while their work is aimed at the university and college student, you will find their message is very relevant to everyone for the cause of Christ. Other organizations such as Inter-Varsity, Young Life, Youth for Christ and the Navigators will be able to recommend speakers available in your area.

You might want to write several book publishing houses and ask if there are any writer-speakers in your area. And certainly you would want to use your own church missionary, if one is at home on furlough. However, of all these sources, the very best is word-of-mouth questioning. Keep a list of who said what to whom. Our memory is so filled with other responsibilities that three weeks after we have heard a good speaker we cannot remember her name, so keep a list for future reference.

Contacting the Speaker

I know how you would like to schedule a good speaker — right after she's spoken and right on the spot. But most speakers I know do not carry a complete date book with them at all times. So often after I've sung and spoken someone has said, "Can you come to our banquet next year in May on the first Thursday?" So exhausted am I that I can hardly remember my name, much less what I'm doing next year on the first Thursday in May. Generally speaking, it's not too good an idea to pounce on a speaker with a future date after she has just finished a program. Rather, ask her if you can get in touch with her for a future engagement. Give her pencil and paper (I can never find either) and have her give you her address or phone number.

Phoning the Speaker

I wish I had a dime for all the phone calls I've received that included a guessing game like this:

"Hello."

"Hello, is this Joyce Langendorf?"

"Yes, this is Joyce Landorf."

"Well, we would like to know if you are able to come to our banquet and sing and speak?"

"May I ask who is calling?"

"This is Mrs. Smith." (Now there's a big help. I know five Smiths.)

"Mrs. Smith, what church are you calling for?"

"The First Baptist." (Another big help. I know 26 Baptist churches in this Los Angeles area alone.)

"Which city, Mrs. Smith?"

"Oh, 'So and So' city. Don't you remember me? Four years ago you spoke at the church around the corner and I met you and asked if someday you would come to our church. You gave me your phone number and I've just been elected chairman and we want you to come." (She sounds just a little wounded because I didn't recognize her by her voice.)

"How nice to talk with you again. Now what date did you have in mind?"

On and on it goes. I end up having to ask about every detail and it always seems the lady calling can't imagine why I'm so inquisitive about her. (Especially since *she* knows *me*.)

Phoning someone is one of the quickest ways of confirming a future date, but by all means follow some of these rules.

1. Identify yourself even if you have met the speaker. You may feel closely akin to a speaker after she has spoken, or you may have seen her or read her books, but it's a one-sided arrangement because she has not had much opportunity to see and talk to you, except perhaps briefly and under hectic conditions. Just as I was writing this I looked up one week in this year's round of banquets. With 350 people attending Monday night's banquet, 200 on Tuesday, 400 on Thursday, 300 on Friday and 150 on Saturday, it meant that in one week alone, I met over a thousand people — and most all of the thousand felt "as if they know me." I'm glad the Lord helps me to communicate like this, but it's hard on a speaker to try and remember all those people and names.

Once a lady asked, "Don't you remember me?" I confessed I didn't and she said, "Oh, but I met you at Phil Kerr's musical one night four years ago." Three thousand people were there that night, and three hundred came back stage! So *do* give your name clearly, your organization or position, your church and what city.

2. State what type of program you are aiming for and some of your goals for that date. Include any special details such as if it's for men and women or mothers and daughters, etc.

3. Specify what financial arrangements can be made. (More on this later.)

4. Give the date or a choice of several, if your speaker

is in much demand. It will save you a second phone call if you have a couple of dates in mind.

5. Be brief. It saves both parties time and money.

Writing the Speaker

This has been the first year for me to have a secretary, and all I know is that God knew I wouldn't last much longer without one and as He answered my prayers, my secretary says He answered *her* prayer, but I think my request was in first since I've been praying about it for five years.

The volume of mail connected with 25 banquets a year is phenomenal and I only wish I had saved some of the priceless correspondence I've received. Some of it has been meticulously typed, while others left everything to my own imagination, including a return address. Sometimes the letter was written so business-like it was almost hostile; others sounded like a genuine "fan" letter, but almost every letter was written by a chairman who really wanted to do her best. Sincerity seems to be the theme in each letter.

Here is an excellent example of how a confirmation letter should be written, and I took it from my files this year as it covers everything from dates, places and goals, to finances.

Yorba Linda, Calif.
March 15, 1967

Dear Mrs. Landorf:

I am writing to you concerning our Mother & Daughter Banquet which is scheduled for May 12, 6:30 P.M. I contacted you by telephone back in September and you said you would reserve this date for us. You suggested that I write a letter of confirmation in March and let you know some of the details.

The banquet will be held in our rather antiquated, but large social hall. We tentatively plan to have the piano (low spinet type) on a raised platform so that you can be well seen and heard from the whole room. Our theme concerns "Reflections," that is to say, the importance of reflecting Christ in our lives because our daughters will reflect what they see in us, etc. . . . I have heard you relate ideas similar to this in your "Notebook" and know you can give a meaningful message concerning this. We plan to invite women from other churches to insure a good crowd, and the "little" gals will adjourn to the nursery for the program.

We are also trying to incorporate a fashion show of home-sewn garments in our program, as we have many mothers and high school girls who sew.

I hope this makes sense and you can get an idea of what our program will consist of. We want it to be really enjoyable and at the same time meaningful for Christ, and we know that with your help it will be. It would be of help to us if we could know in advance how much you charge. We realize it's not an easy thing for you to be driving long distances for programs, particularly at night.

If you have any questions, I trust you will contact me.

Sincerely, and in the Lord's service,

Pat Rath, President
United Society of Friends Women
Yorba Linda Friends Church
4842 Main St.
Yorba Linda, Calif. 92686

Her letter the next month, combined directions (I have no sense of direction) and a request for pictures. Again, this letter is a perfect guideline.

Yorba Linda, Calif.
April 17, 1967

Dear Joyce,

Thank you for your letter of confirmation.

As for directions, I believe you will find it easy to find Yorba Linda by going down to the Corona Freeway and taking the Carbon Canyon Road until you reach Imperial Highway. Go left on Imperial Hwy to Yorba Linda (just 2 or 3 miles). It angles through town, so you take a sharp turn *left* on Main Street. Main St. is exactly one block long and the Friends Church is next to the Bank of America. I don't think you will have any trouble as it will still be daylight. In looking at the map, Yorba Linda appears to be directly south of where you live.

We are deep in our planning and enthusiasm, and really looking forward to meeting you. We would very much appreciate 4 or 5 pictures of you for our advertising if you have them available.

In His service . . .
Pat Rath

Most of my letters of "direction" leave much to be desired and I wish program chairmen were as honest as Bonnie Lanz of Garden Grove, California when she wrote, "My directions aren't so hot, so I asked my husband for the best route for you." (Bless her.)

If you are planning to draw a map, try to remember north is always at the top of the paper (unless it's at the side). One chairman wrote directions and said she didn't know the name of the street, but "You turn right at the second Shell gas station after the Alpha Beta market on your left. It sits a little behind the root beer place." All I saw behind the root beer stand were the garbage cans. I never *did* figure out what she meant, but I did find the place, and what's better, I was on time. Of course, I vividly remember the chairman who told me to turn right on River Street and it turned out that River Street was under construction and not only was it not marked, it wasn't even there! (I wasn't on time to that one.)

I've come to the conclusion that most women have gone to their church 10 to 20 years and haven't the faintest idea *how* they get there each time, and should someone steal the gas station on the corner or the big billboard on the left, they would probably miss church by 50 miles. (I'm just as bad at telling someone how to find my church.)

If I haven't met a chairman in person, then somewhere in our letters she will say she is looking forward to meeting me. One such expression came from a harassed, busy chairman named Marilyn Morsch, who wrote: "I am looking forward to meeting you in person and believe me, the day after I intend to collapse on the couch and do nothing!" That should give you some clue as to how tiring my personality can be. Letters like this one turn out to be great fun and I had much opportunity to kid Marilyn about it.

Finances

Now here is the most touchy, misunderstood subject in the world, but most of the touchiness and misunderstanding could be cleared up if everyone were not so afraid of bringing it up. One minister's letter to me regarding a concert date said beautifully, "I never hesitate or feel embarrassed to ask what financial arrangements should be made. Please feel free to discuss this with me." Another letter said, "We do not know what your fee is, but we do have a small budget. Please give us a suggested fee and we will try to make it satisfactory for your time and effort."

Most of the speakers I know really appreciate this kind of honesty and forthrightness when talking about

LET'S HAVE A BANQUET

money. None of us want to "charge" but any other arrangement is unfair and unrealistic.

Recently a syndicated advice column printed a letter about paying a minister for the funeral. The letter-writer said that the minister should not be paid in money because he was called of God, but a silent prayer of thanksgiving should have been enough. The answer from the columnist made me really smile, as my dad is a minister. The columnist said that if men who are "called of God" don't pay their bills, they may be "called" by the credit bureau and the answer ended with the thought that "thanksgiving prayers" don't put food on the table or pay any bills.

I remember the lady who asked me to speak at her church some 50 miles away from my home. Since she did not mention finances I asked, "Can you tell me if you have a budget for speakers or some other financial arrangements?" After what must have been the longest pause on record, she said stiffly, "We do not *pay* anyone. God supplies all needs and you know God answers in much more than *mere* money." She did have a point, so I went the 50 miles, sang and spoke, and I did not receive a cent, but I did get one pat on the back and three "God bless you's." The fifty-mile ride home was a lonely and tiring ride, but it gave me a chance to think about this whole business of being paid. I began to go over the events of that day.

First of all, I had picked up my suit from the cleaners. (I made it two years ago at a cost of $6.00.) The shop's owner, a lovely Christian, said, "Well, I hear you are speaking tonight out at such-and-such. My sister goes to that church. The Lord bless you, and that will be $3.50 for the cleaning." When I went to the gas station, the attendant and owner, a Christian in our church, said, "If you are going to go many miles more on those tires, you're in for trouble . . . and that will be $3.75 for the gas."

All the way home I kept thinking, if the Scripture was true about a workman being worth his hire, and surely all the workmen I had encountered that day were well worth their hire, and I had paid them with real green money — why wasn't I paid with real green money? The situation reached a new height when I got home and my babysitter said, "I prayed for you tonight as you went to speak, and my fee is $1.75." You see, in theory it works very well for us to pat someone on the back and tell them they are to do this "as unto the Lord," but it's rather one-sided and it doesn't go very far at the grocery store (even though the man there is a Christian too).

A chairman of one banquet said to me, "Isn't this wonderful! All the food was given, the decorations and even the prizes were donated as unto the Lord." I thought, *Yes, that's true. They were given, but somewhere along the line someone paid (in cash or credit) for each item, because* money *is the medium of exchange.*

When it comes to the speaker, she speaks "as unto the Lord," but somewhere along the line she pays for tires, gas, clothes, books and babysitting, and she pays with *money.*

I am all too aware of Christian artists and ministers who abuse the privilege of being paid and insist on outrageous honorariums. But the majority of dedicated men and women who serve year in and year out are grossly underpaid. Too many Christians feel the pastor should not be paid very much, but put the same shoe on the foot of the Christian and not only will they disagree, but they probably won't even tithe. Better yet, ask any Christian electrician, plumber, doctor or lawyer for their services and tell them they should give their talents as unto the Lord, and I'm sure they will not see it quite your way.

I stated earlier in this chapter that much of this problem could be cleared up by frankly discussing it between both parties. Here is a classic example of what happens when you don't want to bring it up and the chairman certainly doesn't want to either. I count this as one of the most priceless (pardon the pun) experiences of my life.

When the chairman called me for her mother and daughter banquet she didn't discuss finances and I thought that surely she *wouldn't* have me come, sing and speak and *not* give some kind of honorarium, so I said nothing and we made no financial arrangements, but settled on a date. The dinner was about half over when the chairman turned to me and said, "Do you expect to be paid for this?" Her tone of voice was about as gentle as a hit with a baseball bat, and for a second I just sat there looking quite stupid, and still chewing my creamed chicken. I recovered enough to ask her if she had a budget or a speakers' fund. She replied with a simple, "No." Then, without another word to me, she got up from her chair, took her spoon, tapped on a glass of water for attention and said, "I'm going to put a little basket at the back door and anything you want to put in it will go to our speaker." My face registered three shades of blush as she calmly sat down and finished off her dessert.

After I had sung, spoken and shaken hands with all two hundred women, I found myself face to face with the chairman — and what to my wondering ears did I hear her say but, "Will $1.36 be enough?"

My husband said that evening, ". . . and you took it?" Well, actually I wasn't to the point of being cyanotic (that's a medical term for turning blue), but a definite *type* of shock had set in and I vaguely remember dumping the change into my purse and coming home. I suppose I really should have talked this over with the chairman (as I have advised you to do). But, come to think of it, I would have missed this remarkable experience.

Should you not be able to pay your speaker the night of her date with you, be sure to tell her that a check will be in the mail the next morning and then *back that up.* Famous last words many speakers hear are, "Our treasurer is not here tonight, but we will send you the check in the morning." Somehow that "morning" never comes.

Should you have to be late with a check, here is a letter sent to me a week after an engagement, and it is very well said:

Dear Joyce:

Thank you for your delightful music and inspiring message last Friday evening at our church.

We did enjoy your visit with us and I'm sure I speak for all.

This is also an apology . . . our president requested a check from the church treasurer, who happens to be my husband. He did not mention it to me because the money had not been given to him, and "No money, no checkee," as he says.

So, do forgive the delay in receiving your well-deserved remuneration.

May the Lord bless you and yours above all you could ask or think.

Yours in Christ,
Marjorie

One other word on finances: If your church is a very small church and you *really* cannot pay a speaker's suggested honorarium, tell the speaker what you *can* do. Most of us will bend over backwards if you are willing to take care of some of the costs. I do several concerts and speaking engagements each month where little or no money is exchanged and I do it cheerfully. But to take advantage of a speaker and expect her to come many, many miles and give of her time for no remuneration at all is very unfair and certainly not in line with Christian behavior. I think it is very interesting that quite often a small church is more generous and appreciative than a large church. After I have turned back their hard-earned money I have experienced that lovely assurance that God indeed does pay in much more than "mere money."

The Gracious Touch

This is the part of this book I have been eagerly awaiting, because here is where I can share some of the marvelous, wonderful things program chairmen all over Southern California have showered on me. At the beginning of the book I stated that these women are a most admirable group and I have learned many lessons from them. How true this is!

I deeply feel that Christian women should be the most gracious women in the world. They also should be the most beautiful (I don't necessarily mean "beautiful" in the present day concept of the word), the most charming and the most individualistic women ever seen or heard because of the miracle of Christ. For how precious it is when the Holy Spirit enters a rebellious woman, ugly with the anger her rebellion has stirred, and transforms even her facial expressions into a gentle beauty. I have seen Him take a domineering woman and transform her loud brashness into quiet efficiency. Where she was going off in nineteen uncoordinated ways at once, she now handles nineteen things, all in their good time and good order by the presence of the Holy Spirit and by putting the proper goals first. I have seen Him take a widow, lonely and shut up in her house, and watched with wonder as He revealed a plan for her; a plan that could only be for her for it involved other widows and soon her life was full again and once more she was beautiful.

Most of the chairmen I know have experienced the gracious touch of God's forgiveness in their lives and then have gone about sharing the gracious touch with all they meet. Listed below are some of the gracious, thoughtful things they have shared with me, and I have seen the reflections of Christ and His matchless beauty in all of them.

1. *Guests*

The gracious touch starts with a letter weeks in advance of the banquet like this one.

Dear Joyce:

Our church wants you to know you can bring a guest to the banquet. Please let us know so we can arrange seating at the head table. I should have mentioned this in my previous letters, so forgive my oversight.

Sincerely in Christ,
Marjorie

Certainly the trips I have taken over the past years have been made easier by some friend or relative coming with me. It's not too bad to be lost on a freeway if someone is along to help misread signs with you, but getting lost by yourself is pretty grim.

I was talking with another speaker, Ruth, about the courtesy of a chairman letting you bring a guest for the long trip. She told me one of her experiences. She had asked a certain chairman is she could bring a guest. The chairman had said yes, so a friend drove Ruth to the banquet. During the meal, Ruth wasn't sure if she was to pay for her friend's dinner or not so she said to the chairman, "Shall I pay for my friend's ticket?" The chairman answered, "Yes, it's $1.75." Ruth pulled out $2.00 and apologized for not having any change. The chairman said she didn't have any either and didn't volunteer to get some, so Ruth finally said, "Well, keep the $2.00." "All right," answered the chairman as she tucked the money into her purse!

I hardly need to say this because I know none of you reading this would be that thoughtless — but you can't possibly know what it means to a speaker to take a guest with her. Usually the committee takes care of the ticket. I will always be in debt to the lovely chairmen who have extended this courtesy to me.

2. *The Maze*

Time and time again, I have pulled into a parking lot

and begun the exciting search for the banquet. I say it's exciting because I've had all kinds of adventures while trying to find everybody. You can't always tell where the dinner is going to be held simply by following the delicious smell of food cooking, because that just might be the night dinner is to be catered and the trucks haven't yet arrived. So, you go in one door, up a stairway and down a hall because the lady you are following seems to know where she's going. However, as it turns out, she knew where she was going, but you find yourself in the nursery child-care room still looking for the banquet.

Some churches hold their banquets in the main sanctuary of the church and this is not too hard to find, but I have attended dinners that were two blocks away from the parking lot (and across the street) so it's usually quite a puzzle.

The gracious touch happens when the chairman tells me in advance that someone will be *out on the parking lot* to meet me. How wonderful it has been to pull into a lot and have not only someone stationed there to meet me, but a parking spot near the entrance marked for my car. This may sound like a terribly little thing, but it is the little things that do make the big differences.

Several years ago, when my face was not quite so familiar, I had many interesting times trying to get to the head table or just trying to attract the attention of the busy chairman. One such time came when I arrived a little early. The door to the banquet hall was open and people were still rushing madly around, so I thought I would simply tell the nervous program chairman that I had arrived and then I would quietly sit in some corner and collect myself. A lady in a red dress whizzed past me, so I called out to ask her if she could direct me to the chairman. She didn't answer and she didn't stop. The second time she started toward me I said, "Could you tell . . ." She looked at me but didn't see a ticket in my hand, so she said, "If you don't have a ticket, I can't help you." Before I could answer she had whizzed past again.

Since I was getting tired holding my Bible, song book and about ten albums of mine, I just walked over to the side of the room and sat down. About 15 minutes later it was obvious that everyone was getting a little anxious as to the whereabouts of the speaker, but no one had spoken to me (or asked about the ticket), so I decided to see what they would do (especially the lady in red).

I was still sitting by the wall as the table in front of me filled, and a dear elderly lady said, "My, I don't think I know your name, are you with someone?"

I was so grateful that she had spoken to me, I must have sounded unusually gushy as I thanked her. When I told her my name, she left me quickly to get the pastor's wife. The pastor's wife turned out to be (you guessed it) the lady in red! Her first words to me were, ". . . if I'd known *who* you were, I would have taken you to the head table."

Why is it that we can't be friendly or plain courteous *before* we know *who* someone is? I was given the red-carpet treatment by the pastor's wife, but by then it was a little late. I would have gladly settled for a friendly "hello" about twenty minutes earlier.

On another occasion, the pastor's wife and two hostesses met me at the entrance as they did everyone else coming in, and then they just motioned for me to go up the stairs, turn left (or is it right?) and "we'll see you later." Everyone was talking with their own friends or relatives, and the few I could get to say "hello" back to me said it and then returned to their conversations.

The gracious touch is exemplified by the chairman or hostess who makes the speaker feel at ease by taking her to the waiting place, room or table. I'll never forget the chairman who assigned a lovely hostess to me who in turn took me to the ladies' room, let me get freshened up and pinned the corsage on me while we were there (so we could both see what she was pinning) and included a little tour of their facilities while we waited for dinner.

This kind of a hostess assigned to the speaker is a huge help to the busy chairman, for she can relieve the chairman of making small talk while so many details must be taken care of. The hostess can introduce the speaker to the people of the church and even run interference if necessary. This hostess could be the pastor's wife, an acquaintance of the speaker, or your most gracious member of the congregation, but what a joy she can be for the ease of your speaker. Writing as a speaker, I'd like to add that with this kind of help and introduction, it is easier for us to do a better job all the way around.

3. *Dinner*

With skirts getting shorter every year, the most frequent question I hear at a head table is, "Does the tablecloth come down on the other side?" This is no joke, but a very serious problem, especially when the head table is on a raised platform. If you do not have a cloth long enough to cover the front side, a covering of white paper will do nicely.

The head table is always served first for two reasons. First, courtesy demands it since it is the "head" table. Honored guests, chairmen and various officers are seated there. Second, if the head table is served first, obviously the guests are through first and the program can be started, giving the speaker a moment of breathing time before she speaks.

The gracious touch comes (and when this happens it always delights and surprises me) if the lovely centerpiece on the head table is given to the speaker. Many a night I have come home weary and tired from the drive, but the beautiful flowers or decorative centerpiece that has been given to me has lifted all my sagging spirits. On our entry hall table is a lovely plastic flower arrangement from last year and it still fills me with warmth as I remember the gracious people who gave it to me.

4. *The Program*

There usually isn't too much time between the dinner and the program, but the few seconds that do exist should be well spent. Sitting at the head table and eating fried chicken does disastrous things to your lipstick and your hands, so this is the moment when every speaker would love to have had the following experience.

The fried chicken was good, but since most etiquette authorities agree you can pick chicken up with your fingers, it did make quite a mess. (I was wondering how it would look when I played the piano with my fingers sticking to the keys.) Everybody at the head table was trying to wipe their fingers clean and a few had started to repair the damage done to their lipstick. (I think women look particularly unattractive when they take out their little cosmetic case and begin a repair job in front of everybody.) I was just wondering what I would do when the pastor's wife asked me to come along with her. She led my friend Sheila and me upstairs and into the pastor's private office and then showed us the private rest room. She left saying she would be back in a minute or two. By the time she returned, it had been just enough minutes to get washed and refreshed . . . and have a moment of "pulling my thoughts together" — so very needed after a busy hour of talking and fellowshiping around the table.

The pastor's wife then did something that no other church, chairman, or pastor's wife had ever done in my five years of this kind of banquet. She took us into her husband's office and asked to have a moment of prayer. As she began to pray, I thought how incredible this was. I had prayed with a pastor before almost every concert I had given, but never, never with anyone before a banquet program. I can't explain why not, unless it is because of the business of getting a program together, or the lack of time. But to my way of thinking, no time of prayer was ever more important. The moments of prayer settled my heart as well as the food, and God was able to bring clearly into focus exactly what He wanted me to share with the dear people waiting in the main sanctuary. It was one of the most gracious touches and I'm sure I accomplished much more for the cause of Christ because of those precious moments.

I told another pastor's wife about this experience, so at their mother and daughter banquet she took the speaker to the rest room and then to the office for prayer. I called the speaker the next day to ask how the evening went and all she could tell me was how thrilling it was for the pastor's wife to have prayed with her. (Funny thing about that!) It was no wonder that many hearts were reached for Christ that night.

Once in a great while I come across a minister's wife who has some real obstacles or problems in her Christian life. I remember one who was polite, but not in the least friendly. Praying with her would have never accomplished the work of the Holy Spirit for the audience, but it may have started a transforming work in her. I was disappointed that I missed an opportunity to witness, for I should have insisted on our having a few moments of prayer together.

5. *After the Program*

Once a program is over, my mind doesn't actually leave me, but it does tend to be a little incoherent and vague. It helps so much if a chairman (or maybe the same hostess that was assigned to you in the beginning) can stand by and help with introductions and the receiving line. Some people want to give their thanks, others have questions (in condensing I sometimes leave sentences unfinished) and some need not only Christ, but some practical and scriptural advice for every day. I know I am not too brilliant after a long program, but the Holy Spirit is never fatigued and many a life has been challenged and changed by a word — even in a reception line! A good, alert hostess can hustle an over-lengthy talker along or hold the line while a speaker talks over a needed point with someone.

If your speaker has recording albums or books with her, people will want copies, so have someone sell them for her as this will be an enormous help. The speaker can autograph copies as she chats, but to sell, talk and write is a herculean task.

After many programs, it has been my joy and extreme pleasure to talk privately with hundreds of women about their relationship to Christ. I've watched God come in and transform a heart. I've watched Him give deep, settled peace in the midst of an overwhelming heartache. I've watched Him replace rebellion with real beauty and love on the face of a teenager, and I've watched Him melt a bitter, angry spirit by His forgiving love. I am sure His plan will always work out. But deep in my heart I know that the love, work, prayers and graciousness of the chairman in these little timely things have freed me to be the speaker God wants, and have encouraged me to give to the banquet my all and my best.

5

The Main Event

or "Help!"

Books

Never before in any age or year have I seen so many "how-to" books. You can buy or borrow books on everything from how to do your own plumbing, electrical wiring or interior decorating, to how to raise orchids, strawberries or French poodles. Certainly there are many books to help you with menus, table favors and decoration and party ideas. (Zondervan even has an *Encyclopedia of Party Ideas*.) So check your bookstores and libraries, then skim as many books as possible, for often you can take an idea from one book and adapt it very well to your budget, your committee and your program.

One of my friends spotted me under the dryer the other day and asked about this writing. She laughed when I told her it was a "collection of events," and said, "Have you included the banquet at our church where you were left completely alone at the head table for the first fifteen minutes of dinner?"

"No, as a matter of fact, I'd forgotten *that* event."

I'm not sure how I managed to forget it as it was a

rather strange experience sitting at that long head table all alone and facing a whole church full of people.

Then we began to talk seriously about this book, and she asked if I told how to cook for several hundred people.

I checked several cookbooks and found, to name just two, *Better Homes and Gardens Cook Book*, published by Meredith Publishing Company, and *Meals from the Manse Cookbook*, published by Zondervan. Both have sections on how much food per person and can sizes you'll need for quantity cooking. The library will lend assistance here, for there are books with complete recipes for 50, 100 or 400 people.

It's always very refreshing to find a woman who is willing to admit that she doesn't know absolutely everything and therefore doesn't hesitate to ask questions, read books and do lots of research for the cause of Christ. Over and over again, each chairman tells me that a positive attitude is the most important quality for a chairman to have. Certainly it begins here — checking all kinds of sources with an open mind and a heart sensitive to what God would have for your group.

As you have your daily devotions and are reading God's Word (the greatest "idea" and "how-to" book), ask the Lord for just the right passage of Scripture to use as the foundation stone for your program. At this point there is always someone who says, "But Joyce, I'm so busy I can't find time for regular devotions each day." All I can answer is that you will never *find* the time for it, as the time will never be there. And may I hasten to add that, if you are too busy to have this time each day, you are entirely too busy. I always have believed that reading and prayer is the vital link between God and man, between victory and defeat. But when it came right down to actually practicing it — ah . . . *that* was another story. Nine out of ten Christians agree on this, but only *one* out of ten actually does it.

My own lack of devotions was pointed out sharply to me by a book called *My Spiritual Diary* by Dale Evans Rogers. I always excused my lack of devotions because I was so busy, but as I read Dale's book, I realized over and over again that *my* schedule was not nearly as involved as *hers*, and she not only kept her appointments with God, but wrote a book about it to boot! Tell me your schedule and I'll find someone who is busier and still finds time for devotions.

You see, we *will* keep that time if we exercise the four-letter word *obey*. Obedience to God is by far the most difficult job in the Christian life. Henrietta Mears said she never had to *lose* her will, only to *train* it to obey. It may well be that while you are reading the precious Word of God, the right verse and the right thought will come, and that lovely still voice of God will begin rolling the first wheels of inspiration towards its destination — your banquet.

Prayer

In our choir repertoire is a song called "Teach Me to Pray." One day after we had sung it, a man asked our director why he had chosen such a song. "We don't need to be taught to pray, we should just pray," he stated flatly. The choir director then reminded him of the disciples who asked Jesus how to pray. Why, if it's not necessary to be taught, did they ask? We really need to be *taught* so we will be asking in accordance with God's will (as James tells us).

Martha Snell Nicholson, in her book *Wings and Sky*, has one of the loveliest poems on prayer I have ever read. You will understand it best if you read it slowly and aloud.

OUR MINISTRY

All power, all love,
All knowledge Thine;
What need hast Thou
For prayer of mine?

We cannot tell,
We only know
We have Thy Word
That it is so,

Co-workers we
With Thee, our King!
What songs of praise
My heart would sing,

That prayer from me,
Of little worth,
May win a soul,
May move the earth,

May haste the day
Of Thy return!
The fires which on
Thine altars burn

My hands may tend
Until that Day! . . .
Teach me, O teach me
How to pray!

We always have that small gnawing feeling that our little insignificant prayer is not going to make much difference one way or another. Yet the Scriptures tell a much different story. Prayer *does* make the difference and just how much you underestimate the power of prayer is just how far your program is going to miss the mark of success.

It is my prayer for you that God will teach you how to pray for your people and your program so that you will not pray amiss or pray out of the will of God. How important your own daily prayer life will be in these planning months. Who knows, maybe this will be a very big growing experience for you, and who knows (except our Lord) what the harvest will bring?

People

We often hear quoted, "No man is an island unto himself." We know the truth of this, for no one truly lives alone. Many of us try our best to be blasé and sophisticated to the point where we *think* we don't need others, but we always have and we always will.

The early Christians with no lovely church sanctuaries and grand educational units, were admonished to gather together, to have the fellowship of each other's friendship and to be strengthened by each other's words. As the song says, "people need people." We need the prayers, the love, and yes, even the criticism of people. People can be a far bigger asset to your chairmanship than you dream.

You may want to use the idea of a questionnaire in finding out all kinds of things about the people with whom you will work or serve. The women of Bethany Baptist

Church of Whittier, California, did just that with a unique sheet of questions. Beside each question was a darling little drawing (mimeograph-type), and at their mother and daughter banquet every woman had one of these sheets at her plate. She was told just to fill it out and leave it on the table. Here's how it read:

THAT WE MAY INVOLVE ALL WOMEN!

We want to better know *you* — your *interests*, your *desires*; so that we might make our Women's Mission Society meaningful, *active, alive* & *alert* to the needs of *all women!*

Will you please "pencil check" *one* or *more* of the areas below and return to your Women's Missionary Fellowship president.

WOMEN'S MISSIONARY FELLOWSHIP
BETHANY BAPTIST CHURCH
Whittier, Calif.

Name _____

Address_____ Phone_____

1) I'm a "new chick" but a "lone duck" . . . haven't gotten acquainted but would like to. Would be interested in joining a circle.
2) I've been a little "slow" in becoming active, would now be interested in circle participation and becoming an "active member."
3) I have a "nest full" at home and can't attend day meetings. Besides I need a night out! (Hubby could baby-sit.)
4) I'm also a "young mother" of "Jr. Women." I'd pre-

fer a "morning circle" at the church where we could have a baby-sitter for all.

5) My "little ones" come home from school early so I'd prefer a "morning circle."

6) I'd prefer a "night meeting" . . . for no other reason than . . . I'm a "nite owl!"

7) I'm a "working woman" with limited time. I'd like a Business & Professional Circle that's "on the ball! (Night meeting, of course.)

8) Nothing wrong with "eating" . . . if you like "pot-lucks" and such . . . just say so!

9) I'm interested in a "sewing circle." White Cross work is my interest, and would like to be in a circle that does lots of "sewing."

10) I'm interested in community service projects . . . Christian social relations and what we as a group can do in these areas. I'd like circles to be formed by "interest groups."

11) I am interested in a church service circle. I'd like to come once a month and clean the kitchen or work at addressing envelopes, or wherever they would need me.

13) I think we should forget circles and have just real bang-up fellowship meetings for all the women.

13) Please leave me alone — I'm not interested!

This questionnaire, done with a sense of humor, can be of vital help for your year of planning.

People can make the difference as far as prayer goes too. Whom would you call if the most shocking, tragic, or happy thing happened? If you are like me, you would probably call a Christian and preferably a *praying* Christian. One Christian praying friend is worth a thousand non-praying friends. Time after time I hear someone say,

"I don't know what I would have done without those people praying for me!"

When my mother passed away a few months ago, I lost not only my mother, but my dearest "praying friend." Since then I've seen a wonder-working God in action and to my delight and joy, I've new "praying friends" to help take her place.

Stop right now and ask yourself, "How many people do I know whom I could call any hour (day or night) with any kind of shocking, embarrassing or sordid story and ask for their prayers?" Probably only the fingers on one hand would reveal your *real* praying friends — friends who wouldn't be shocked or angered and who would go quietly to the throne of God for you. How important this kind of friend can be to your success in the Christian life. I praise God for the few (very few) friends who pray daily for me, and I consider them my biggest assets in helping me to achieve God's purpose in my life.

FRIENDS

O precious friends, who hold me up
In prayer, I could not drain my cup,
I could not walk this thorny road
Did you not plead for me to God!

How sweet and strange this gift of prayer!
You know my need and voice my care
And speak for me before His throne;
He reaches down, that Holy One

To smooth the road before my feet;
And thus the circle is complete!
Dear friends of mine, I never knew
That I would owe so much to you!
— MARTHA SNELL NICHOLSON

Don't be afraid to seek the advice, love and prayers of others for your banquet as it may turn out to be a miraculous, exciting and fruitful time for everyone because of them. God uses all kinds, shapes and sizes of people for all kinds of uses — but use us *He does*.

There is a famous legend concerning the Lord after His resurrection and His return to heaven. The legend says He was met at the gates by the angels and they were all excited to know about the work He had left here on earth. In questioning Him, one angel finally combined all their thoughts.

"Dear Lord, whom did you leave in charge of the work there?"

"Eleven men," He answered.

They were shocked. "Only eleven men?" they cried, "But Lord, what if those eleven men fail?"

"Then I have no other plan."

This may be just a legend, but the point is very true. God uses you (His women) to carry the Great Commission from your street and your next door neighbor to the remotest tribe of Africa or South America. He will use you if you will let Him and He will use you according to your faith, according to your desire to obey and according to your willingness to let the Holy Spirit work. This is what makes a Christian's life so exciting to live — there is no limit to what God can or will do in your life.

Can you catch the vision of yourself in this role of chairman? Not *just* a chairman, not *just* decorations chairman, not *just* the mistress of ceremonies, not *just* the cook, not *just* part of the program, but a woman doing what God wants her to do, a woman giving God her very, very best.

So, let's have a banquet. And, no, a dollar thirty-six

will not be enough. It's not enough for the meal, decorations, or the speaker. It's not enough for originality, planning or hours spent working. You see, a great banquet will cost everything you can give it! It's this way with every worthwhile project in life — if it's well done. It is going to cost, and a high price will be paid.

My hat is off, I'm waving at you and I'm shouting all my best wishes as you take on your new position of chairman. But look out, once you really master this business of being a chairman and become very efficient in it, the year is over and guess what? Some darling gal stayed away from the meeting on election night, was elected as chairman, and you are out of a job! However, fixed firmly in your heart forever are the near tragic mishaps of such-and-such a banquet, the memory of all those working and planning sessions, the last minute changes that turned your hair a little gray; and finally, topping it all, are the wonderfully rewarding memories that only a gal centering her life in Christ can have. God *Himself* has given her a rich field and the harvest has been truly magnificent!

LET'S HAVE A BANQUET!